LESSONS
FROM THE
DISABLED
LIST

DEVOTIONS
FOR
ATHLETES

ELLIOT JOHNSON

Lessons from the Disabled List

Elliot Johnson, Lessons from the Disabled List

ISBN 1-929478-19-4

Cross Training Publishing
P.O. Box 1541
Grand Island, NE 68802
(800) 430-8588

This book is manufactured in the United States of America.
Library of Congress Cataloging in Publication Data in Progress.

Cross Training Publishing
P.O. Box 1541
Grand Island, NE 68802
1-800-430-8588

The print appearing on the cover is "Vintage Yankee Yarn"
@ Bill Williams
Bill Goff Inc.
P.O. Box 977
Kent, OH 06757

Contents

Chapter Three • COLOSSIANS

Chapter Four • 1 TIMOTHY

Foreword

MAJOR LEAGUE BASEBALL TEAMS have a place for those who are injured and unable to play. It's called the "disabled list." The player is not eligible to play, though he still is the property of the team. This list is temporary, and whenever the player is well, he is activated.

The Romans thought they had put the apostle Paul on a "disabled list" when they imprisoned him. But in 62 ad, he sent some of the greatest letters ever written to the far reaches of the empire to believers in the Lord Jesus Christ. Tychicus, Epaphroditus, and Onesimus carried mail to the Ephesians, the Colossians, and the Philippians. These letters were used by God to build and reinforce his team! Under God's inspiration, Paul used his time on the "disabled list" in Rome to write some of the most influential letters that have ever been written.

In 64 AD, Paul was temporarily taken off the "D. L," and was released prison. He wrote to Pastor Timothy in Ephesus and to Pastor Titus on Crete, giving God's wisdom for leadership in the churches. When rearrested, Paul again wrote to Timothy just before he was killed by the Romans for his faith.

What a leader was Paul! And what a Savior he followed! May these letters be used by the Spirit of God to encourage and strengthen you, whether you roam free or are on the D.L. in century 21!

EPHESIANS
Introduction

EPHESUS WAS A PROSPEROUS SEAPORT of 340,000 on the Aegean Sea. Here was located a beautiful temple dedicated to the pagan goddess Diana (Artimis to the Greeks). This temple, four times the size of the Parthenon, was one of the seven wonders of the ancient world. It was the scene of vulgar sexual rituals in worship of Diana, goddess of fertility. Paul had visited Ephesus twice, the second time for a three-year stay. He had won many converts to the Lord Jesus. The craftsmen who made idols lost so much business that they rioted and threw Paul out of town (Acts 19)!

The theme of Paul's letter is Christ as Head of His body, the church. Chapters 1-3 tell us who we are in Christ. They speak of our *position*. Chapters 4-6 tell us how to live accordingly. They speak of our *practice*. We sit with Him in heavenly position. We are to walk with Him in a way that is worthy of that position. And we are to *stand* against our enemy, Satan. Paul had warned the leaders of the Ephesian church to beware of false teachers from without and professing believers from within who would teach perverse things (Acts 20:29-30). They had avoided false teachers, but their love for Christ would later grow cold (Revelation 2:2). Paul wanted it to stay red hot and he was a great example — even from the disabled list!

Untold Wealth

Praise be to the God and Father of our Lord Jesus Christ, who has blessed us in the heavenly realms with every spiritual blessing in Christ.

Ephesians 1:3

THE MATERIAL WEALTH of many Americans is almost beyond belief. So are their priorities! In 1997, a public auction of Mickey Mantle's memorabilia was held in New York. Wealthy fans paid $6,900 for a lock of Mantle's hair, $9,200 for his passport, and $7,175 for his American Express card. A copy of his last public speech brought $24,150!

The wealth of believers in Jesus Christ is truly beyond measure, but our priorities are much different from the average American's! We have already received both grace (God's undeserved, unearned favor) and peace from Almighty God! Yet, Paul knew we all need fresh grace daily to remain at inner peace in a world of turmoil! "In Christ" (not "in Adam" or "in Artimis") we have every spiritual blessing we could ever receive! So we needn't seek spiritual blessings from other sources. There is nothing as wonderful as being "in Christ." Everyone in the world is either "in Adam" or "in Christ." If we are "in Adam" we are lost, but to be "in Christ" is to be saved! Those "in Christ" are accepted and favored by God forever! As long as God accepts Christ, He accepts and favors those "in Christ."

Blessing means "to benefit or to prosper." We must enjoy the blessings we possess! We were chosen, made holy, forgiven, predestined to be adopted as God's sons, and redeemed! All of this is free! As believers, we need not ask for these things. God has already given them to us! They are based upon the selection of the Father (vs 4-6), the sacrifice of the Son (vs 7-12), and the seal of the Holy Spirit (vs 13-14).

First, we were chosen by God. Salvation is an act of God, not of man. Man is responsible to believe God (v 13), but it is God who elected us to be saved before He created the world! We will be holy and blameless before God! Notice, God never

10

elected anyone to be lost. Anyone who refuses Christ is lost because he wants to be lost. After we are saved, we are pre-destined to be adopted into God's family and given the rights of an adult child of God, just as the Greeks gave a son the full rights of sonship in the ceremony known as the "toga virilis." God could have saved us without making us His sons, but He chose to do both. Since He has done so by grace, we certainly should praise Him!

After God the Father planned our salvation, Jesus the Son came to earth to redeem us and form His church with nail-pierced hands. We are redeemed. This means we are delivered from slavery to sin (false steps or transgressions). It cost the blood of Jesus to deliver us. He alone gives us wisdom (objective insight) and understanding (subjective apprehension) of His grace. Redemption (Gr. "apolutrosis") as used here means "to liberate by the payment of a ransom in order to set a person free." Redemption ("agorazo") in 1 Corinthians 6:20 means "to buy in the marketplace." Redemption ("exagorazo") in Galatians 3:13 means "to buy and to keep for one's own use, never to sell again." But redemption in Ephesians 1:7 has all three meanings! Jesus has bought us out of slavery in the marketplace of sin, never to sell us again, but to set us free of our sin!

We are redeemed through His blood. 1 Peter 1:18-19 says ""For you know that it was not with perishable things such as silver or gold that you were redeemed from the empty way of life handed down to you from your forefathers, but with the precious blood of Christ, a lamb without blemish or defect." One drop of the precious blood of Jesus can save every sinner ever born on earth! Redemption costs the shedding of blood. Hebrews 9:22 says, ". . . without the shedding of blood there is no forgiveness." When man forgives, he merely wipes out the debt another man owes him. But God is holy and righteous and His forgiveness demands a price to be paid. Jesus paid that price!

It is becoming more clear how wealthy we are in the riches that really matter! Some Americans have wealth to throw away on the personal effects of dead baseball stars, but believers in Jesus Christ have eternal, heavenly wealth! No words can describe the wealth we have in Him! And no one can rob us of this wealth! Hallelujah!

Read Ephesians 1:9-14

The Purpose of God

And he made known to us the mystery of his will according to his good pleasure, which he purposed in Christ, to be put into effect when the times will have reached their fulfillment — to bring all things in heaven and on earth together under one head, even Christ.

Ephesians 1:9-10

UNLIKE RACE HORSES, greyhounds have no rider. They chase a mechanical rabbit made of fur! A few years ago at a track in Florida, an electrical short caused the rabbit to stop in the middle of a race, explode, and go up in flames! The confused dogs didn't know what to do. Several stopped and laid down with their tongues hanging out. Two dogs ran into a wall and broke ribs, another began chasing his tail, and the rest howled at the crowd! Not one dog finished the race! All had lost purpose in running.

God has a purpose for every created person, place and thing for both time and for eternity. Almighty God has revealed His purpose to man! His purpose will never be short circuited, like the mechanical rabbit. God's mystery (formerly concealed but now made plain) is that all things everywhere are going to be brought together under one Head — the Lord Jesus Christ! This will happen when the "times" we are now living in are fulfilled. When He has achieved His purpose in our times, God will place Jesus on the throne of the earth and everyone everywhere will submit to His Lordship! This mystery can only be discovered by the revelation of God. Man could never figure out the purpose of God on his own!

Heaven and earth are not in harmony today. When Mark McGuire hit his 62nd home run in 1998, the game was delayed, a huge ceremony was held, and the capacity crowd cheered him loud and long. If Jesus Christ Himself had appeared and stood in the middle of the stage in St. Louis, would the cheering have been so intense? No! Most people despise the risen Savior today. Wicked men shake their fists in the face of our holy God. But one day, every knee will bow before Him! God has decreed it to happen and He will work it out according to His will (v 11).

Both Jewish (v 12) and Gentile believers in Jesus (v 13) are included in Christ! Any man, woman, or child of any skin color, language, or nationality who trusts Christ as personal Savior is permanently marked with a seal — the Holy Spirit — which guarantees his or her inheritance. The baptism of the Holy Spirit, which occurs the moment one believes in Jesus, is God's "down payment" on that inheritance! The entire purpose of our salvation and for all creation is "to the praise of His glory." We exist for God's glory! We are to bring praise to Him. He has taken us into His confidence and revealed the goal towards which all history is moving.

We now know who we are, why we are here, and where we are going. Only believers in Jesus can answer these basic questions of human existence. We exist for the glory of God! What a great purpose for living!

Read Ephesians 1:15-23

Worthwhile Knowledge

. . . so that you may know him better.

Ephesians 1:17

BOB DOLE NEEDED TO KNOW baseball better. Or maybe he forgot what he knew. In 1996, while addressing a crowd in Los Angeles, Dole predicted he would win the presidency by comparing himself to Hideo Nomo, who had thrown a no-hitter the previous night.

"The Brooklyn Dodgers had a no-hitter last night and I'm going to do what Nomo did and we're going to wipe them out," said the politician. The Dodgers had left Brooklyn for Los Angeles thirty-eight years earlier!

Though the Ephesians were not without faults, they represented the early church at its best. Though they had been given all spiritual blessings in Christ, Paul prayed continually for them after they had been saved. He prayed that they would increase in their experiential knowledge of

God. Matthew Henry says that Satan gains control of his people via their passions and senses, but Jesus gains control of us via our deeper understanding of God! The knowledge of God is gained by revelation of God. It is more worthwhile to gain in understanding of God than to gain any new scientific discovery! Sadly, most people don't value the knowledge of our mighty God. Even most Christians are ignorant and unappreciative of their spiritual possessions! The knowledge of God is not apprehended by academic wisdom. It is gained by meditating upon God and His Word and by experiencing His dealings with us.

We should grow in the knowledge of our sure hope — the fact that we will reign with Jesus over this universe! We should gain knowledge of Heaven, our true inheritance. We should gain knowledge of God's mighty power. It's the extraordinary power God used to raise Jesus from the dead and to cause Him to ascend to Heaven! This is the greatest power known to man! It is irresistible! No one can ever complain of a lack of power to meet temptations, to live each day, or to share Christ with others. God's power is stronger than any addiction, lust, or fear. Anyone who has little power has spent little time with Jesus and His Word.

Angels and demons have varying degrees of power. Jesus has infinite power! He rules over all, but He is not flexing His muscles just yet (Hebrews 2:8). He is the head of His body (the church), which is made up of all born again believers in Jesus. The true church is a living organism, not a dead organization. It is the fullness of Christ, for whoever heard of a King without a kingdom?

Emerson said, "Know thyself." Paul says, "Know God!" To know Christ and the power of His resurrection, to share Christ's sufferings, to become like Him, and to rise from the dead were the ultimate for Paul (Philippians 3:10). Are they that important to you?

Read Ephesians 2:1-10

From Rags to Riches

But because of his great love for us, God, who is rich in mercy, made us alive with Christ even when we were dead in transgressions — it is by grace you have been saved.

Ephesians 2:4-5

YOUNG JOCKEY EDDIE ARCARO went from rags to riches. After 250 unsuccessful rides, the 15-year-old finally won his first race at the Agua Caliente Racetrack in Mexico on January 14, 1932. Eddie had 4,778 more victories in a famed career that lasted until 1962. He won five Kentucky Derbys, six Preakness titles, and six Belmont Stakes!

All who have trusted Christ as Savior have gone from rags to riches in the spiritual realm! At one time, we were all dead. We were not weakened, not sick and not merely disabled — we were dead! We had no victory. We were spiritual corpses in Death Valley! Indeed, everyone without Christ is a walking dead man. To be dead means to be cut off from God. All sinners outside of Christ are devoid of the ability to reason concerning anything spiritual. Now, all sinners are not as bad (in practice) as they might be, for some commit more heinous outward acts than others. But all sinners outside of Christ are as bad off as they could be. They are condemned by God to eternity in hell. Everyone who sins (any form of wrongdoing in thought, word, or deed) is included!

All sinners continually follow the evil ways of this sick world. The world system ("kosmos") is a Satanically organized system that hates and opposes God. This world has what the natural man craves. It offers the money, pleasure, and power sought by men. No one seeks God of his own determination. All naturally seek self-gratification. Anyone who is saved is saved because he is drawn to God by the Holy Spirit. He never sought God on his own!

All sinners follow Satan, the god of this age (2 Corinthians 4:4). The human race has forsaken the true God, embraced the lies of Satan, and descended into terrible depravity (Romans 1:18-3:20). Some even live lower than animals in their behavior. They are merely doing what comes naturally. The god of this age controls sinners in three ways: via the lust of the flesh, the lust of the eyes, and the pride of life (1 John 2:15-17).

All sinners are objects of God's wrath. Our righteous God has a holy displeasure with sin, without which He would not be the moral Governor of His universe. This righteous indignation is revealed against all sinners now and will climax with the last Judgment. It is a terrible thing to be under the wrath of God.

Thankfully, God didn't leave mankind in his pitiful situation! *Because* of His love, *out of* His great mercy and *by* His grace God made all who receive Jesus to be alive! He loves all! He loved us while we were sinners (Romans 5:8). He is full of mercy. But it took grace to save such vile creatures who had sinned against His love and mercy. God could have annihilated Adam and Eve and turned paradise over to the angels with a clear conscience. But He had grace toward us! The works of man's hands cannot save him. His religious ceremonies or rituals are insufficient. It takes the blood of God's Son, Jesus, for us to be saved. Salvation is not repairing the old nature of man. It is creating a new man! Adam and Eve must have been heartsick when they realized what a horrible thing they had done. But God mercifully turned death into life! He immediately promised a Redeemer! Mercy means we didn't get what we deserve. God takes no pleasure in the death of the wicked. He rejoices to pardon every sinner who repents and believes on His wonderful Son!

When we repent, God gives us Christ's righteousness! He raises us from the dead and our present *position* is "seated with Christ in the heavenly realms." Now, our present daily *practice* will match our position! Our future is to "display the incomparable riches of his grace" in the coming ages! William McDonald says that heaven will be a school for us and for the angels. God is the teacher and His grace is the curriculum. The term is for eternity! But we will never know it all, for only God knows everything. As we get to know God now, we taste heaven!

Salvation is entirely by the grace of God. Man can do nothing to obtain it except to believe God by faith. We struggle against this truth, like a drowning man who cannot swim and must trust himself totally to his rescuer. Our misguided efforts to save ourselves only keep God from saving us! God's grace is the means and our faith is the channel of salvation. He couldn't save us by His love because He is righteous and sin demands a penalty. Jesus paid that penalty! That's grace! Salvation is a gift, so we cannot boast of it! There will be no boasting in heaven, because there will be no one there with anything to boast about! Only Jesus can boast. We worship Him. If you could be saved by your own works, you would be a Savior and you could worship yourself! But Jesus is the *only* Savior!

Having believed in Jesus, we were "recreated" by God. We were not reformed, repaired, overhauled or retrained — we were made anew! "Born again" is the phrase. We are new creatures (2 Corinthians 5:17). We are His workmanship (Gr. poiema = "poem"). What a piece of work we are!

The good things we do result from His recreative work in us. He created us to do good works. His works are performed in and through us. God has a spiritual blueprint for every life. He gives us the ability, energy, and opportunity to do good works for His glory. What a Savior! What a rags to riches story!

Read Ephesians 2:11-22

The Wall Comes Down

For he himself is our peace, who has made the two one and has destroyed the barrier, the dividing wall of hostility.

Ephesians 2:14

PEOPLE OF DIFFERENT NATIONALITIES and colors have created walls between themselves. Everyone knows of the abuse heaped upon Jackie Robinson, baseball's first black player in 1947. But in 1951, Wally Yonamine, an American of Japanese descent, played his first game with Tokyo's Yomiuri Giants. He received the same harsh treatment from fans in Japan. He also played like Robinson, beating out teammate Tetshuaru "The God of Batting" Hawakami for three batting titles.

Even though Jesus had said, "I have other sheep what are not of this sheep pen" and "I must bring them also" (John 10:16), the Jews had erected a dividing wall between themselves and non-Jews (Gentiles). God had revealed Himself to the world through the Jewish nation, desiring that they invite Gentiles into the family of God. But the Jews failed to keep God's law, rejected the Messiah, and claimed racial and religious superiority over "Gentile dogs." They manifested great racial hatred when Jesus came into the world. Refusing to deal with Gentiles, they prayed each day they would never see the face of one!

The Gentiles were cut off from God and without hope of eternal life. Gentiles had gods who couldn't see nor hear. Epicures and Aristotle did not believe in any future life. Platonists said we'd be happy, then miserable. Stoics thought we'd all cease to exist at death. All were far from God and truth. They had none of the Old Testament promises made to Israel.

But the blood of Christ changed everything! We are not brought near to God by converting to Judaism, by doing our own work, or being circumcised or baptized. We are brought near to God by the blood of Christ. Jesus is our peace. He brings peace with God and peace between Jew and Gentile. Nationality, skin color, wealth, poverty, gender, social position and educational differences all fade into insignificance. He has made all believers to be one body.

In the temple was a five-foot stone wall keeping Gentiles from coming into the inner court where Jews could worship. A sign warned Gentiles to stay out upon penalty of death! God destroyed that wall of separation. Today, we are God's building, His dwelling place. God doesn't dwell in a structure with a steeple. Jesus Christ is the "Chief Cornerstone" of His structure, the body of each believer!

The cross is the remedy for all racism, segregation, and bigotry, and governments will never solve racial discrimination. Only Jesus can do it! The unsaved man has a heart that is a spiritual garbage can. He needs a new heart. God does not make us better men, but *new* men. All believers are now first class "fellow citizens" and members of God's family. God's household is built on the foundation laid by New Testament apostles (missionaries) and prophets (those who forthtell the Word of God to strengthen people). The entire building must be lined up with Jesus as the standard. We are "in Him" and He is "in us." The wall has fallen down! Praise His holy Name!

Read Ephesians 3:1-13

The Gentiles and a Mystery

. . . .this grace was given me: to preach to the Gentiles the unsearchable riches of Christ, and to make plain to everyone the administration of this mystery, which for ages past was kept hidden in God, who created all things.

Ephesians 3:8-9

YEARS AGO, TWO YOUNG BOYS were hitchhiking to Milwaukee's County Stadium for a Braves' game. A car pulled over and the driver called out, "Where are you going?"

"To the ballpark," they replied.

"Hop in," the motorist said.

As they climbed into the car they were overcome with joy. The driver who had called them was future Hall-of-Fame pitcher Warren Spahn on his way to the clubhouse!

The apostle Paul was called, too. In Ephesians 3, he began to explain his call. He said God had revealed to him by direct revelation that Jews and Gentiles together would make up the chosen people of God! The all-wise God had withheld this information in the Old Testament, but He revealed it to New Testament apostles and prophets. The mystery was not that Gentiles would be saved, for Isaiah had predicted that many times (11:10, 42:6, 49:6, 56:6-7, 60:3), as had other prophets. The mystery, so hard for Jews to accept, was that Gentiles would be included as equals in one body, the church! This is the theme of Paul's prison epistles. He considered himself the least of all God's people, and he was in a Roman prison because of false charges that he had taken Trophimus, an Ephesian Gentile, into the temple area in Jerusalem which was reserved for Jews (Acts 21:27-32).

God had made Paul a minister to proclaim the unsearchable (unfathomable) riches of Christ. Words fail to explain

19

Christ. He is the eternal Creator, the Sustainer of all life, the Almighty and Glorious King of the universe. Yet, he became poor to demonstrate His unselfish kindness and generosity. He was crucified and resurrected for us! God's purpose was to reveal His great wisdom to rulers and authorities (angels and demons) in the heavenly realms. What a plan! Peter says angels long to look into the incredible nature of God's plan (1 Peter 1:12). God is their Teacher. His many-faceted wisdom (like a kaleidoscope) is the lesson. The universe is the classroom and angels are the students! They marvel at His eternal purpose, for He knew everything would happen just as it had happened before He created anything and He had a detailed plan that is progressing just as He ordained! They marvel at His triumph over sin. They wonder over His sending heaven's Best on behalf of earth's worst. He has redeemed His bitter enemies, conquering us by His love and grace. He is transforming us for His glory and He will take us to heaven to honor us for eternity!

Therefore, through Jesus we may approach God confidently. He delights to have us come to Him to share sorrows, joys, and requests. We have "freedom of speech" before Him! We must not be discouraged over suffering, for there is purpose behind it all. Even though Paul was on the "disabled list" in prison, he refused to despair. What a God and what a plan!

Read Ephesians 3:14-21

A Reason to Pray

For this reason I kneel before the Father . . .

Ephesians 3:14

STUDENTS AT COLUMBINE HIGH SCHOOL, especially athletes and Christians, had great reason to pray when killers Eric Harris and Dylan Klebold shouted, "All jocks stand up! We're going to kill every one of you." They proceeded to kill 12 students and a teacher, including Cassie Bernall, who was shot for confessing, "Yes, I believe," when asked if she believed in God.

Paul had a strong reason to pray for the Ephesians. Because they were now part of God's household (2:19) and Paul was concerned they not become discouraged (3:13), hc prayed that they might be strengthened (to overcome) with a dynamic power (Gr. "dynamis") by the Holy Spirit. He prayed to the Father of all redeemed ones in heaven and on earth. He prayed that Christ might dwell (be completely comfortable) in their hearts by faith (not by feeling). He prayed that they might be rooted (nourished as a plant) and established as a building in the love of God. He prayed that they might have power to grasp more of the dimensions of God's love. He prayed that they might know this love that surpasses knowledge! What an impossible task without the revelation of God! He prayed that they would be filled to full capacity with God and he closed his prayer with a great doxology of praise to God.

Is Christ at home in your heart? Is He comfortable with every thought, word, deed, book you read, TV show you watch, video game you play, food you eat, and money you spend? Is Jesus in complete control? Or is He just a guest or occasional visitor? In some people, Jesus is merely *present* and others He is *prominent.* But in still other believers Jesus is *pre-eminent!*

Do you realize His love is as wide as the entire world, as long as eternity past through eternity future, as deep as the lowest depths of any man's sin, and as high as our heavenly home? His love is like an ocean without shores. His love enables Jew to love Gentile, blacks to love whites, and whites to love blacks.

Unto Him (not to us) be glory in the church (the body) and in Christ Jesus (the Head) forever! He can do exceedingly abundantly above all we ask or even imagine! We can leave the final outcome of our lives to Him, for He is wise and more powerful. When we let Him be Lord of all, we are full of God and we enjoy His love! What a way to live! What a Savior to which we pray!

Read Ephesians 4:1-16

Unity — Just Keep It

*Make every effort to keep the unity of the Spirit through the
bond of peace.*

Ephesians 4:3

TEAM CHEMISTRY IS ESSENTIAL to success. That's a big
reason why the Dodgers signed 41-year-old Orel Heischiser for
2 million dollars for the 2000 season. Despite one of baseball's
highest payrolls in 1999, the Dodgers finished 77-85, good for
third place in the NL West. "We lacked some leadership, we
lacked the right chemistry . . ." said general manager Kevin
Malone. "We've got to make the necessary changes."

Team unity is as important in the spiritual realm as in the
athletic realm. The Spirit of God has given us (Jew and Gentile) unity as believers in Jesus and Paul tells us to make
every effort to keep it. There is enough of our old nature
present to ruin any church or project of God! We must sub-
merge petty, personal whims and attitudes. A good slogan is,
"In essentials, unity; in nonessentials, liberty; in all things,
charity."

Paul would have been a great football coach. He urges us
to be humble. Humility was not found in Greek culture,
except among slaves. As the opposite of conceit and arro-
gance, it was not valued. He urges us to be gentle, submitting
to God's dealings and man's unkindness. Meekness is not
weakness, but "restrained strength." It means "power under
control." He urges patience (an "even disposition under prolonged provocation"). We are to "bear with one another in
love." We must love those who irritate, disturb, or embarrass
us. These are not commands to earn our salvation or to pay
God back for our salvation. Our high position simply calls for
godly conduct!

God has made us as one body. There are no denomina-
tions in Heaven! One Spirit indwells all believers. We believers
all have one hope — to be with and like Jesus one day! We
have one Lord (Jesus!), one faith (the gospel given once for
all), one baptism (which proclaims our unity), and one God

and Father. Therefore, Jesus said call no man on earth, "Father" in a spiritual sense (Matthew 23:9)!

When Jesus ascended to heaven, He provided gifted men to build up His body. There were diverse kinds and amounts of gifts which promote unity. Apostles performed miracles to confirm the message (2 Corinthians 12:12). They carried the gospel by God's authority. Prophets received direct revelation from God to build and encourage the church. Evangelists explained the gospel, answered objections, encouraged repentance, and gave assurance to new believers. Pastors ("shepherds") counseled, corrected, encouraged and consoled their flocks. Teachers explained, interpreted, and applied Scripture. All believers were (and are) in full time Christian ministry. A great hindrance to the gospel has been the separation of "clergy" and "laity" roles. The purpose of using these gifts (and others listed elsewhere in Scripture) is to equip the saints to serve God, to build others up, to unify Christ's body, to know God better, and to grow up spiritually. Then believers won't be immature, unstable (going from one religious fad to another) and gullible.

Speaking "truth in love" is the key to growth. As a living organism, the church grows naturally when all use their gifts. It heals (renews) itself as the nutrition of the Word of God is digested. Every believer is needed, so there is no stunted spiritual growth. When "Lone Ranger" Christians abound, we suffer from "spiritual dwarfism." Are you using your gift to benefit Christ's body? If not, you suffer along with the rest!

Read Ephesians 4:17-24

Saintly Living — Now!

. . . put off your old self, which is being corrupted by its deceitful desires; . . . and put on the new self, created to be like God in true righteousness and holiness.

Ephesians 4:22-24

ALMOST 2000 YEARS AGO, Augustan of North Africa heard the message of the gospel and was drawn toward it. But not quite willing to forsake all his vices, he prayed, "Lord, make me a saint. But don't be in a big hurry about it!"

Augustan couldn't have it both ways. He couldn't be a saint and live like a sinner. When Paul wrote to the Ephesians who had trusted Christ, he insisted that they live up to their high calling — now! He urged them to make a clean break with the old life, which they had led as unbelievers in Jesus. Paul describes the life of sin as *futile*. Sinners are under the empty illusion that there is satisfaction in sin. It's like aimlessly chasing bubbles which burst into nothingness or shadows that disappear in the light. Unrepentant sinners have a *darkened understanding*. Being blind to truth, they have lost the perception of moral values. Many Americans wouldn't recognize a moral value if it punched them in the nose! They are *separated* far from God because of their *ignorance*. Just as some drink up an entire paycheck, wake up with a splitting headache the next morning, and call it "partying," the Ephesians were ignorant because of their hard hearts. Their seared consciences no long restrained them. They had gotten over the original pain of offending a loving God with their sin. They were *insensitive, sensual, impure,* and *lustful*. The sexual sins of their lifestyles are basic sins of unbelievers in our own culture. These "deceitful desires" enslave people and God allows their sin to become their punishment (Romans 1:24)! Their unbridled lusts become their executioners!

Believers in Jesus are crucified, dead, and buried with Him and raised to live radically new lives! Saved people put off their old nature like a dirty coat and put on Christ's life like a new one. We listen to His voice and obey Him. Our attitudes toward sin are different. We now *hate* the old life we used to live. Every day our old nature resembles a decaying corpse, decomposing more and more. We don't reform, renew, or repair that corpse. We consider it dead and buried!

Have you "put on" the Lord Jesus Christ and become a new person? Or are you like Augustan, wanting to be good — someday? Better do it today. It may be now — or never!

Read Ephesians 4:25-32

Tear Away Jersey

Therefore, each of you must put off falsehood and speak truth-fully to his neighbor . . .

Ephesians 4:25

SEVERAL YEARS AGO, TEAR AWAY JERSEYS were popular in college football. It wasn't uncommon for running backs to go through two or more per game. The light fabrics would tear when grabbed by a tackler and prevent "shirt tail" tackles. Sometimes the jersey hung in ragged strips before a player went to the sidelines for a replacement.

Paul writes that each Christian is to remove the tattered and torn "jersey" of his old life. Lying is first mentioned. All of us are guilty (Psalm 116:11). Every deception and dishonesty in personal relationships, business deals, and government negotiations must be put off. We must especially not lie to other believers, for we are members of the same body. Our eyes wouldn't lie to our hands about where the ball is as we tried to catch it! If we lie to other members of the body, we hurt ourselves! Jacob's life is a good example of self-inflicted suffering, for he lied and schemed against his own family.

Persistent anger must also be removed from our lives. Anger is not wrong, for God is angry every day (Psalm 7:11). He relents the moment people repent. We must "cool off" quickly by making Christ-like adjustments to irritating cir-cumstances. Prolonged anger allows Satan to gain a foothold in one's life and lead us into further sin. We must control anger before it controls us!

Bandits roamed the mountains around Ephesus, and Paul lists "stealing" as the next vice to avoid. We must avoid every theft from grand larceny to unpaid bills, copyright violations and falsifying expense accounts. We are told to work so we can give to others as well as to help our own families.

Unwholesome ("rotten") talk only tears others down. Hunter says it is "the index of a dirty mind." Roustino adds, "If a rotten word is found in the mind, shut it off at the mouth." Shady stories and frivolous, empty conversation

25

grieves the Holy Spirit. He is the one who sealed us in Christ. Our security in Christ is a strong reason we should not sin! When the Holy Spirit is grieved, He doesn't use us and the world doesn't believe we really are God's children.

Next, Paul mentions the emotional sins of bitterness (inward resentment and hardness), rage (rapid, boiling outbursts of temper), anger (smoldering indignation), brawling (loud outbursts), slander (abrasive insults), and every form of malice (from a viscous disposition to ill will towards others). We must take off these sins like a torn jersey.

The jersey Jesus gives us is one of kindness (gentle, unselfish concern for others), compassion (tender mercy), and forgiveness (freely, fully and finally forgetting the sins of others) for Christ's sake. He forgave us, so we can forgive others. Wear Jesus' jersey. It looks much better than your own!

Read Ephesians 5:1-7

Jesus Jersey

Be imitators of God, therefore, as dearly loved children.

Ephesians 5:1

WHEN A PLAYER IS A MEMBER of a team he must wear the jersey of the team. The jersey identifies him as part of the team. He represents the team. His teammates know him and so does the opponent. It would be foolish for a player to expect to get into any game if he refused to wear the team jersey!

Christians must wear "Jesus Jerseys" if they expect to be effective in the game of life. They are identified as belonging to Jesus by their resemblance to Him. Love and sacrifice for others are the identifying features of a "Jesus Jersey." Because we are loved by God, we can love others. Because He gave Himself for us, we can sacrifice for the benefit of others.

In putting on a "Jesus Jersey," we must take off the old jersey of the world. This means there is no place for sexual immorality, impurity, greed, obscenity, foolish talk, or coarse joking.

26

Sexual immorality means all sex outside of marriage. It relates to pornography. There is even danger in speaking lightly and familiarly of such conduct in a way that lessens the sinful character of such deeds. 2 Timothy 2:19 says, "Everyone who confesses the name of the Lord must turn away from wickedness." This includes impurity of all kinds.

Greed is worship of things instead of God. Greed is "high treason" against the King of kings. Obscenity is shameless talk and conduct. Foolish talk means "empty conversation worthy of a moron." Coarse joking means a "vulgar wit." Don't bring sin into your mind by frequently discussing it. William McDonald says that doing so brings you closer to doing it! It is dangerous to joke about sin. The world's attitude is that immorality is acceptable. God calls it sin. We are to have thankfulness in our minds, which brings real satisfaction.

McDonald says that the immoral, impure and greedy are idolaters for three reasons. First, they have a wrong concept of God. He *never* approves of immorality. Secondly, they worship the creature above the Creator. Third, they put their desires above God's will. Immoral, impure and greedy people may claim to be Christians, but they are not saved and their lives prove it. God's wrath comes upon such people. His attitude toward sexual immorality is seen in Numbers 25:1-9, where He killed 24,000 Israelites because of this sin. His attitude toward homosexuality is seen in Genesis 19:24-28 where he rained fire and brimstone upon cities filled with brazen homosexuals. The natural judgments of AIDS, mental breakdowns, and emotional disorders are included in God's judgment upon such sin. Believers are to have no part of such evil behavior. When Satan (or a false teacher) approves of such vile conduct by saying, "You shall not surely die" (Genesis 3:4), God says, "The wages of sin is death" (Romans 6:23). No child of God lives in such evil. "Jesus Jerseys" look and fit so much better!

Read Ephesians 5:8-14

Light Wins

For you were once darkness, but now you are light in the Lord.
Ephesians 5:8

SUNDIALS WORK GREAT when the sun is shining. But at
night time, they tell nothing. People in darkness can take
their own flashlights and make a sundial record any time they
desire. But only the sun tells the truth!

Our world is in terrible darkness and lost people do
whatever is right in their own opinions. But only the light of
God's Word is truth. All of us were once darkness before we
were converted. But, all who come to Christ are enlightened.
The saved know they are saved because now they are light in
a dark world. Just as one can tell the difference when his eyes
are opened or closed, so the saved see the difference between
spiritual light and darkness.

The fruit of light is goodness (moral excellence), righteousness (integrity), and truth (honesty, sincerity). These things
are seldom sought, flattering to others, comfortable, or popular in a dark world. The saved try to find out what pleases
Jesus. Every conversation, article of clothing, book, pleasure,
business deal, friendship, recreation, piece of property, and
sport is examined to see how it appears to Him.

We have no fellowship with works of darkness. Even to
mention the terrible sins done secretly is shameful. Believers
expose these deeds of darkness by their holy living, which is
in stark contrast to the evil around us. Just as light dispels
darkness, not by lecturing but by its presence, so the presence of Christians brings light to the darkness around us.
Sometimes, under the guidance of the Holy Spirit, we use
words When the light of Christians is dim, the culture grows
even darker.

Our lives are to constantly be preaching a sermon, extend-
ing an invitation to others to "come to the light." In the Old
Testament, Israel was told to wake up and be light to all
nations. Isaiah 60:1-3 says, "Arise, shine, for your light has
come, and the glory of the Lord rises upon you. See, darkness

28

covers the earth and thick darkness is over the peoples, but the Lord rises upon you and his glory appears over you. Nations will come to your light, and kings to the brightness of your dawn."

Christian, wake up! If we wake up and shine the light of Christ upon our dark world, friends will be saved and our nation will be restored! Light will win over the darkness.

Read Ephesians 5:15-21

Dominated

Do not get drunk on wine which leads to debauchery. Instead, be filled with the Spirit.

Ephesians 5:18

NOTRE DAME DOMINATED college football from 1946 to 1949. The Irish never lost a game, won three national championships, had two Heisman Trophy winners, and sent more players to pro football than any other team. Some sports writers said the country's second best team was their second unit!

If believers in Jesus would let the Holy Spirit dominate their lives like Notre Dame dominated college football, this would be a different world!

Paul says we are not to be totally dominated or controlled by selfish desires, by others, or by wine. We are to be filled (controlled) by the Holy Spirit! Worldly men and women are unwise and foolish. As God's children, we are to be wise, making the most of every opportunity. It is a sin to waste time, for God won't strive to seek men's repentance forever. Earth's opportunities to earn heaven's rewards are limited. The days were evil in Paul's time and Christians were in danger of persecution every hour. The days are evil today, with darkness, difficulty, and death everywhere. We dare not drift aimlessly, but must understand God's will and do it. We must follow God's plan for us as a train follows a track.

Drunkenness in Paul's day was a dominating sin. Devotees of the cult of Dionysus sought communion with God by getting drunk! Drunkenness and use of drugs is still popular.

But drunkenness leads to debauchery ("squandering") your life as the prodigal son squandered his life (Luke 15:13). Instead, we are to be constantly filled with God's Spirit. Like drunkenness, this power for living comes from outside self, makes us fervent in everything and affects our walk! But while wine leads to lack of control, the fruit of the Spirit brings self-control (1 Corinthians 14:32).

We never get more of the Spirit. He gets more of us (John 3:34)! Everyone who knows Jesus is baptized, indwelt, sealed and given the Spirit as a "down payment" ("earnest") on eternity. These are never commanded. They were finalized when we accepted Jesus Christ. But we *are* commanded to *"be filled"* with the Spirit. This is a moment by moment way of submitting to His control. We can be greatly used by God one day and feel empty the next day. We need a fresh filling as surely as our car needs more gasoline! We are filled when we confess all known sin to God, empty ourselves of selfish desires, and yield to His control. It is as much a sin to fail to be filled with the Spirit as it is to be drunk with alcohol!

As a result of being dominated by the Holy Spirit, we will encourage others, be joyful in heart, thank God for everything, and submit to each other. We encourage by speaking Psalms (all were set to music), hymns (composed by men), and spiritual songs. During early days of suffering, Pliny wrote to the brutal emperor Trajan: "They (Christians) want (are accustomed) on a fixed day to meet before daylight (to avoid persecution) and to recite a hymn among themselves by turns, to Christ as if God." The Holy Spirit makes us joyful. He enables us to thank God for everything, for we know He works it all out for good (Romans 8:28). He enables us to submit to each other. This means we are humble, modest, and forgiving — not that we obey every whim of would-be dictators. We won't be selfish in our opinions, rude, or haughty, but will esteem others above self.

All men and women are controlled by something or someone. The control of the Holy Spirit is the only way to live. It is far better than the domination of alcohol, drugs, selfishness, or peer pressure. It is God's will for His Spirit to control us. And He does it for free!

Read Ephesians 5:22-33

Winning at Home

Wives, submit to your husbands as to the Lord . . . Husbands,
love your wives, just as Christ loved the church and gave
himself up for her . . .

Ephesians 5:22, 25

BASEBALL PLAYERS WHO DO NOT KEEP their families
together cannot perform at their best level. Many recent stars
are living proof. The White Sox' Frank Thomas, embroiled in
divorce proceedings in 1998, failed to make the All-Star team
for the first time in six years. Mark Wohlers of the Braves, and
Bret Saberhagen of the Red Sox had their lives torn apart by
divorce that same year. "Being here some days doesn't make a
log of sense," said Saberhagen. His accountant revealed that
he was making thirteen cents on the dollar as a result of his
divorce.

If Christians cannot win at home, they surely cannot win
on the enemy's turf! Our homes are to be symbols of Christ's
relationship with His body, the church. When we fulfill our
roles at home, we win!

What are the roles God has given His team members? God
has put husbands in a place of authority and leadership in
the home. Wives who are filled with the Holy Spirit will submit
to their own husbands. "Submit" is a military term meaning
"to rank under." Though both are of equal *value,* they are not
of equal rank in God's order. When women refuse to be submissive, the marriage becomes a "two-headed monster." This
does not depict Christ and His church.

Submission does not mean the wife is inferior. Jesus is
submissive to the Father, but He is not inferior to Him! If the
husband is not a believer in Jesus, a submissive wife may win
him over (1 Peter 3:1-7)! But submission must be "fitting in
the Lord" (Colossians 3:18). The wife submits first to Christ,
and if ordered to violate His direct commands (to be truthful,
to care for her body, to raise children to honor God, etc.), she
chooses to obey Christ.

31

Husbands who are Spirit-filled love their wives as Christ loved the church. He died for the church (Gr. "ekklesia": an assembly of citizens called out to transact city business")! He loved us sacrifically! He sought our highest good! He died to make us holy ("set apart"), cleanses us of sin, and presents us blameless to Himself. In Eastern weddings, the bride took a ceremonial bath before meeting her groom. Likewise, Jesus cleanses us with *living water* through His *Word* before presenting us "cleaned up" before Him.

Husbands must love their wives as they love themselves, for they are one, completely identified with each other. Men care for themselves, though they be imperfect. Jesus cares for us, though we be imperfect. Husbands are to care for wives, though they be imperfect. He who loves his wife loves himself. They are permanently glued together. To tear them apart is to severely damage both and is often more painful than death. This bond is even stronger than the parent-child bond (v 31).

So, if we want success at home, wives must submit and husbands must love as Christ loved us. That is the game plan of our Master Coach. And His plan always wins!

Read Ephesians 6:1-4

Training Camp at Home

Children obey your parents in the Lord, for this is right.
Ephesians 6:1

PRE-SEASON TRAINING CAMP sets the tone for a football team's entire season. Learning plays and submitting to discipline often dictates how far a team goes in the playoffs. Training camp is not intended to be easy. Discipline and instruction means hard work at all levels. One junior high school athlete wanted to quit football during pre-season training. His father advised, "Wait until after the first game." That first game was so much fun, he never thought of quitting again, and the team went undefeated! The end result was worth the struggle!

Godly parents run a "training camp" in their own homes, though it isn't all drudgery and work! Children are to obey their parents promptly, habitually, and cheerfully. All people of all cultures at all times recognize this as a moral duty. God calls disobedience to parents a sin (Romans 1:30; 2 Timothy 3:2). To honor parents means the child loves and respects them more than the best football coach. This is the first commandment with a promise included: that of a long, prosperous life on earth. Honor brings obedience, which develops self-discipline. Self-discipline brings stability to life. An undisciplined person will probably not live a long life, nor will they prosper. One of the lowest forms of lawlessness on earth is the dishonor of one's own parents. Oliver Greene said, "Never in history have children been so disobedient and disrespectful as in this present day." Samson and Absalom are examples of two boys who did not honor their God-fearing parents, and both died young. They reaped what they sowed.

Children are to obey parents "in the Lord." That is, if ordered to dishonor God by sin (telling lies, stealing, etc.), children are not to obey such orders any more than soldiers should obey orders to slaughter innocent civilians.

The time to begin "home training camp" for children is when they are in the crib. Fathers (and mothers) are responsible to discipline children, but not to exasperate (irritate) them by harshness, selfish displays of authority, petty rules, unreasonable demands, or favoritism. Such provocation makes children feel frustrated and unable to please parents. Children who become discouraged have no passion or ambition in life (Colossians 3:20-21). The Lord is to be the center of child training. Discipline and encouragement must both be prominent. Fathers are more prone to abuse of power, mothers to over-indulgence. Both are wrong. We need God's wisdom at home!

Paul says men must raise children in the training (discipline) and instruction of the Lord. We must teach children the truths of Scripture and live it out before them. Children must not be pampered or catered to. Susanna Wesley said that parents who subdue self-will in children work with God to save their souls, while parents who indulge children do the work of the devil (Proverbs 22:15; 23:13-14; 29:15, 17)! Parents must always be under control but firm when giving discipline to a child.

Training methods must change as the team progresses! At a certain age, spanking becomes ineffective and only exasperates the child. Parents must discern when the child reaches the age when withholding privileges works better than spanking. It's all part of conducting an effective training camp. If training camp is poor, the team suffers the entire season. But if child-training is poor, the child (and parents) suffer their entire lives!

Read Ephesians 6:5-9

Winning at Work

Slaves, obey your earthly masters with respect and fear, and with sincerity of heart, just as you would obey Christ. And Masters, treat your slaves in the same way. Do not threaten them, since you know that he who is both their master and yours is in heaven, and there is no favoritism with him.

Ephesians 6:5, 9

AGAINST HIS MANAGER'S WISHES, Rangers' catcher Pudge Rodriguez arrived late to spring training in 1999. When Hall-of-Famer Johnny Bench was asked how many times he reported late to camp, he replied, "Never. Whatever your job is, you should be on time. Whether it's being on the field or being on the bus or whatever. It's become kind of vogue for guys to have personal matters to attend to before they come to camp. You've got five months between seasons to get that stuff together."

It sounds like Johnny Bench took his obligations at work seriously, just as our Lord has instructed.

God uses the relationship between slaves and masters to direct us, though He does not approve of slavery. The very nature of Christianity condemns slavery, for we are all of equal value in God's sight. Wherever the gospel goes, the abuses of slavery and the slavery itself disappears. None of the world's religions have had the same effect. The gospel dissolves slavery gradually rather than advocating a violent revolution, which always perpetuates hurt and hatred.

Slaves/employees are to obey the bosses' work assignments with respect and fear of offending both them and God. Workers must work sincerely and wholeheartedly. They are to give a day's work for a day's pay without inward resentment.

34

They are to obey as slaves of Christ Himself. In other words, there is no distinction between sacred and secular work for believers. All Christians are in full-time service of Jesus.

Employees who work for Jesus will win the favor of their bosses. They keep the bosses best interest in mind. They never steal from the company by giving goods away or by slacking off. The Lord rewards such workers.

Masters/bosses are to treat workers as God treats us — by rewarding them for good work. They must not threaten them. If American business and labor would follow God's principles, all labor strife would end! A Chinese Christian who was educated in America once said, "It is not that in America Christianity has been tried and found wanting. The problem over there is it has never been tried." May God help both labor and management to obey Him.

Read Ephesians 6:10-18

Armed for Warfare

Put on the full armor of God so that you can take your stand against the devil's schemes.

Ephesians 6:11

WORLD WAR II WAS A BRUTAL CONFLICT to determine whether ruthless dictatorships would rule the world or whether people would be free. The conflict was finally ended in the Pacific because of one of history's biggest discoveries. The University of Chicago had dropped football in 1939. Under their vacant stands, scientists generated the first controlled nuclear chain reaction. When the United States dropped the atomic bomb in 1945, Japan surrendered and the war was finally over.

Like the United States in World War II, believers in Jesus have deadly enemies seeking to destroy them. The world, the flesh and Satan all seek to render us powerless. We must not love the world. We must count ourselves dead to fleshly desires. We must resist Satan. Observing the Roman guards while awaiting trial in prison, Paul writes about the armor we need in spiritual warfare. With every piece in place, we can stand against Satan's attacks, but neglecting just one part of our spiritual armor spells disaster.

Satanic opposition seems to advance and recede in waves, and the Ephesians had been involved with Satanic evil spirits (Acts 19:19). Paul warned them (and us) to stand against the schemes ("methodeias" or "methods") of Satan. The strategies of discouragement, frustration, confusion, moral failure, and doctrinal error have worked for thousands of years to defeat God's people. Satan is experienced, crafty, clever and invisible. He is not a cartoon character in red pajamas with pitchfork and pointed tail. He appears as an angel of light and his servants appear as ministers (2 Corinthians 11:14-15)! He has an organized "spiritual Mafia" on at least four levels. Spiritual "rulers" rule entire nations. Authorities desire to possess humans. "Powers" of this dark world control worldly business, education, and social forces. "Spiritual forces" in the heavenly realms govern religion in the world. Never underestimate the enemy! He knows every deception for which men fall!

Man's weapons are useless against Satan (2 Corinthians 10:3-5). We need God's armor. The belt of truth holds all the armor in place. Truth (integrity) brings freedom, while lies bring bondage. Make friends with truth. Those who speak lies speak the devil's native language!

The breastplate of Christ's righteousness protects us from Satan's accusations (Isaiah 59:17). His righteousness produces moral character and conduct.

The "shoes" of the gospel give us stability. We need this firm power base upon which to base decisions. With gospel shoes, we are prepared to share God's grace with others.

The shield of faith protects the entire body. Roman shields resembled 2 1/2' x 4' doors which stopped darts dipped in pitch and set on fire. Our shield of faith stands between us and the enemy. When someone threatens you, hold up your shield of faith. When they ask a question you can't answer, take the shield of faith until your knowledge increases. Questions about man's origin, God's Word, or suffering in the world have answers from God if we take time to find them.

The helmet of salvation protects our minds. We must be sure of our destiny. No Christian can have peace of mind, encourage others, or resist Satan without assurance of salvation. First John 5:11-13 provides it!

The Roman sword (macharia) was a short, two-edged, razor-sharp weapon. It was so pointed it could pierce armor! No Roman soldier was sent to war until he was an expert swordsman! You must take God's spiritual "sword," His Word, and use it effectively. Study it until you are proficient with it. Your life depends upon it!

Finally, Paul says to pray constantly in the Spirit (1 Thessalonians 5:17). The Spirit of God prays through us, teaching us what to pray. We must pray for all believers, for all of us need prayer in this war. We must stay watchfully alert for Satan's traps and "crack-back" blocks.

We are in a war more intense than the biggest football game ever played. Our enemy has no sympathy. But God's armor is all we need to stand in victory! It gives us greater power than an atomic bomb. By His power, we win!

Read Ephesians 6:19-24

Fearless

Pray that I may declare it (the gospel) fearlessly, as I should.
Ephesians 6:20

NATIONAL LEAGUE PRESIDENT Ford Frick was fearless when he discovered the St. Louis Cardinals were planning a protest strike in 1947 when the Dodgers came to town with Jackie Robinson on the team. He sent this message to the Cardinals:

> "If you do this you will be suspended from the league. You will find that the friends you think you have in the press box will not support you, that you will be outcasts. I do not care if half the league strikes. Those who do it will encounter quick retribution. They will be suspended, and I don't care if it wrecks the National League for five years. This is the United States of America, and one citizen has as much right to play as another. The National League will go down the line with Robinson whatever the consequence."

Though writing from prison, Paul did not request prayer for his release. He asks for bold fearlessness in explaining the gospel! No other topic stirs the emotions and provides such hostility as the gospel. Paul was Jesus' ambassador. Most ambassadors are treated with great respect in the country to which they are assigned. But Paul was abused, chained, and thrown into prison!

We must pray for others, for when we do so we are strengthened, too. Jesus never taught how to preach, but He taught us how to *pray!* We must pray in the Spirit or we are only mouthing words. Sometimes demons hinder prayers (Daniel 10:13). But by persisting in prayer, we can overcome as Daniel overcame. The only way to overcome Satan is to pray without ceasing (1 Thessalonians 5:17). Christians must stand shoulder to shoulder in spiritual warfare and kneel knee to knee in prayer.

Tychicus evidently carried Paul's letter. He was from Asia and tradition says he became a leader in the church at Chalredon. *Grace* opens the letter, is the subject of the letter, and closes the letter to the Ephesians.

PHILIPPIANS
Introduction

PAUL WROTE ONE OF HIS MOST personal, practical, and joy-filled letters to his friends at Phillipi. He was imprisoned in either Rome (61 or 62 AD) or Ephesus (54 AD) when he wrote to thank the believers there for sending Epaphroditus with a monetary gift to make his imprisonment more tolerable. The joy of the Lord in every circumstance comes through loud and clear in the life of Paul.

Philippi was named after Philip of Macedon, father of Alexander the Great. The residents were soldiers and citizens of Rome, forced to settle the area by Anthony (BC 42) and Octavia BC 30) for the protection of the homeland and its borders. The city was famous for gold mines, and being the gateway to Europe, was in a place of danger. In compensation for relocating there, citizens were given all rights of Roman citizens and exempted from taxes.

Though it is in ruins today — Philippi was a miniature Rome. It was the center of Bacchus (God of wine) worship, new-age religion, and Emperor worship. But it also became the birthplace of Christianity in Europe! The story is told in Acts 16 how, in response to a vision, Paul followed God's leading into Europe. He met Lydia, who became the first European convert. He delivered a girl from demon possession, was beaten and jailed, and led the Philippian jailer and his family to Jesus. These people and others formed a church which loved and remained loyal to Paul. Ten years later, Paul wrote this letter of love and joy to the Philippians. His affection for the people remained strong and his joy remained intact. His enthusiasm encouraged the believers as it encourages us today!

Read Philippians 1:1-11

Good Memories

I thank my God every time I remember you.

Philippians 1:3

PAUL WAS A SERVANT owned by Jesus Christ, obedient to Jesus, acting for Jesus, and dependent upon Jesus. He had some wonderful memories. When he thought of the Philippian believers in Jesus, he didn't dwell upon his beating and imprisonment when he was in Philippi ten years earlier. He joyfully remembered their partnership in the gospel! Paul had no business or plans of his own as he wrote to the saints ("set apart ones") in Christ Jesus, the bishops (older saints or spiritual guides) and deacons (servants) in Philippi.

"Grace" ("charis") was the Greek greeting of the day, similar to our "Have a good day." "Peace" ("shalom") was the Hebrew greeting of the day. Peace comes through prayer and thanksgiving. There is never any peace without the grace of God!

Paul was a man of prayer and the joy of the Lord gave him real power in prayer. No wonder God used him! From the very first day he met Lydia and the others at a riverside prayer meeting (Acts 16), the believers in Philippi loved Paul. Possibly the jailer, his family, and the girl who Paul delivered from demon possession were still alive and read this letter!

Paul knew we would never be perfected in this life. But he also knew that Jesus would finish His work in us. We will grow up in Christ, for all living things grow! He always finishes what He begins. Our part is to hunger and thirst for righteousness. Our food is the Word of God (Matthew 4:4), the bread of life (John 6:35) and the living water (John 7:37-39). If he didn't perfect us, it wouldn't get done, for our efforts of self-improvement are futile. We are not mannequins, but living beings! How thankful we are for his persistence in us!

The Philippians had partnered with Paul by giving financial and moral support. As he logically and rationally defended the gospel, they supported him. As he confirmed the gospel by establishing it more firmly in the hearts of believers,

40

they encouraged him. Though he was a Jew and they were Gentiles, all barriers disappeared in Christ. He loved them and they loved him from their hearts.

Paul prayed that their love would overflow more and more with knowledge. Some people are hard to love. In fact, they are unlovable until we get to know them. Paul prayed for the Philippians' increased knowledge. He prayed for their depth of insight. It is vital for believers to have insight in how to love. We must not be naive or gullible in our love of others. We love best when we use sound judgment in how to love others. Paul prayed for discernment in what is best. The good is often the enemy of the best. Some things are essential, others are not essential. We desperately need discernment.

Paul prayed for purity and blamelessness until the day of Christ. He wanted believers to be sincere, real, genuine, and filled with the fruit of righteousness, leaving no room for evil fruit in their lives. The believers' righteousness comes from Christ Jesus. Neither Paul nor the Philippians had any of their own righteousness. Nor do we! Only Jesus is righteous and only He deserves glory and praise! Paul knew it and as we grow in Jesus we will know it, too!

Read Philippians 1:12-30

The Fortune of Misfortune

For me, to live is Christ and to die is gain.

Philippians 1:21

EARL CAMPBELL WAS A LINEBACKER at John Tyler High School in Texas. He felt his position was secure for his senior season. But his coach had other ideas.

"The summer after my junior year, my coach told me we didn't have a running back," Campbell says. "I didn't want to be a running back. I cried like a baby, but I guess that turned out to be a good decision." What Earl thought was misfortune led to a Texas 4A State Championship, the Heisman Trophy at the University of Texas, and the NFL Hall of Fame after eight seasons with the Houston Oilers!

Paul had much misfortune in his life, the latest of which was his imprisonment for two years. This tended to discourage the Philippians. But Paul recognized the sovereign power of God in his beatings, stoning, shipwreck, and incarceration. He served a God who brings good out of evil! Using many descriptive word pictures, Paul wrote that what happened to him advanced ("prokope," i.e. like a pioneer cutting through underbrush) the gospel! The Roman's entire Praetorian Guard heard the gospel, for every four hours another soldier was chained to Paul! The potential to reach 10,000 Imperial bodyguards became reality as God penetrated the royalty of Rome with the Good News! Many guards eventually became Christians, died for their faith, and the Roman Empire was radically changed. Local church leaders fearlessly took Paul's place on the streets when they heard of his confinement. It loosened their tongues for Christ! We have Paul's prison letters today because of his writing from God's "Disabled List." So, Paul was correct in saying he was put there ("keimai," i.e. posted as a sentry) for the defense of the gospel.

There were envious preachers, full of selfish ambition, who wanted to make for themselves a bigger name than Paul's. They saw his effectiveness and wanted some notoriety. Still, Paul rejoiced that Christ was preached! The gospel was winning! Paul wasn't sure whether he would be released or martyred, but he believed the prayers of the Philippians (v 19) would lead to his release. Believing prayer prevailed over the power of the Roman government! He was released not long after writing this letter! But either way, the daily reality of fellowship with Jesus was the most important thing to Paul. More vital than dedication, service, or commitment is personal fellowship with the risen Savior! That's why Paul said, "For to me, to live is Christ . . ." (v 21a). Then he added, " . . . and to die is gain" (v 21b). What we lose at death is gain! To lose our sinful nature, all temptation, every sorrow, all suffering, and all our enemies is great gain! At death, we gain a new, perfect body, the presence of Jesus, total fulfillment, eternal rewards, and a glorious reunion with friends who know Jesus!

There are only two possibilities for believers: to be here on earth or to be with Jesus in heaven (2 Corinthians 5:6-9). As his persecutors led him to his death, one martyr said, "You take a life from me that I cannot keep, and bestow a life upon me that I cannot lose." Paul had mixed emotions about whether he preferred "to depart" (as a vessel weighing anchor or a soldier breaking camp) to be with Jesus, to stay on earth to help satisfy the spiritual needs of others. Epictetus said, "Life is like an Olympic Festival, and we are God's athletes to whom He has given the choice of showing of what stuff we are made."

Whether we live or die, we must conduct ourselves ("live as citizens") in a manner worthy of the gospel. We must contend "as one man" ("synathleo," an athlete as part of a team). "Synathleo" is the origin of our word "athlete." There were violent enemies of the gospel in Philippi. But Paul encouraged the believers not to be frightened (as horses about to stampede). Their fearlessness was a sign of the destruction (not annihilation) of the unbelieving.

For the believers, it was graciously granted them to suffer for Christ. This is the highest privilege in life. Both Paul and the Philippians had engaged in a great struggle ("agon," agony in training) with evil. The contest was real. Real pain was involved. But the joy and victory were just as real, too!

Read Philippians 2:1-11

Overcoming Contention with Humility

Your attitude should be the same as that of Christ Jesus . . .
Philippians 2:5

THE NEBRASKA CORNHUSKERS had two great I-backs in 1982. Senior Roger Craig gracefully moved to fullback, where he carried the ball less and blocked more for Mike Rozier. The San Francisco 49ers noticed his unselfish attitude, as well as his ability and drafted him. Mike Rozier had a good NFL career, but Roger Craig became one of the best NFL running backs of all time. His sacrifice and humility benefited his team, and ultimately himself!

43

Paul would have made a good coach. He wrote about and encouraged humility, unity and teamwork. For four reasons, he encourages the people in Philippi to be one in mind and spirit. The encouragement of unity with Christ, His love, the Spirit of God, and the tenderness and compassion of believers would be enough to unify Christians in spirit and purpose. Humility is the antidote for selfishness and conceit. Placing value on the interests of others instead of selfish ambition corrects our natural self-centeredness.

The Greeks had a dim view of humility, but Christ made it a mark of noble character. Paul quoted an early hymn based upon Isaiah 52 and 53 to demonstrate the humility of our Lord. Jesus is Almighty God (John 5:18) and He was not presumptuous in considering Himself equal with the Father. But He didn't have to "grasp" at being God. He was coequal, coeternal and coexistant with God. He became true man while remaining true God, a mystery we cannot comprehend! He laid aside His expression as Deity in exchange for an expression as a servant. He laid aside His glory, but not His divine nature (John 14:28). He was God, but He didn't walk around with a halo around His head. He was the King, clothed temporarily as a peasant, but He remained the King! He went so far as to accept death, even the cruel death of a humiliating cross reserved for non-Romans and the worst of criminals. Not seeking selfishly to make a name for Himself, He humbled Himself.

Then, God exalted Him. He restored His glory (John 17:5). Everyone will one day confess the earliest Christian creed: "Kyrios Jesus" or "Jesus is Lord!" Every knee will bow before Him (Isaiah 45:23). Colossians 1:20 says He reconciled all things in heaven and on earth, but those who are under the earth are not reconciled.

There are two jobs on earth. One job is man's, the other is God's. Our role is to humble ourselves and Jesus Christ is our example. God's role is to exalt us. If we do our job, He'll do His. But if we insist on exalting ourselves, He'll have to do our job and humble us! It's the only way to have unity on His team.

Read Philippians 2:12-18

Spiritual "Workout"

. . . continue to work out your salvation with fear and trembling, for it is God who works in you to will and to act according to his good pleasure.

Philippians 2:12-13

YEARS AGO, MIAMI COACH DON SHULA was talking to a reporter about a player's mistake in practice. He said, "We never let an error go unchallenged. Uncorrected errors multiply."

The reporter asked, "Isn't there benefit in overlooking one small flaw?"

"What is a small flaw?" Shula replied.

Shula never stopped working the mistakes out of his team. And Christians should never stop working out the salvation that God has worked in them! He has given us the *will* and the *power* to act in ways pleasing to Him. He gave us the mind of Christ, which can not be imitated. His humility is imparted by the Father. As a result of God's work *in* us, He expects good works *out* of us! This is our spiritual "workout," a workout that requires total focus in partnership with Him.

A little girl had trouble understanding how a big Jesus could live inside her if she invited Him into her heart. "Mommy, if Jesus comes to live in me, won't He stick out?" she asked. The answer is "Yes!" Anyone who really has Jesus inside them reveals Jesus continually. Others see Him. People cannot see faith, but they see works as evidence of saving faith. If there are no works, there is no saving faith!

Disputes abounded in Philippi among the followers of Aristotle. But a saved person shouldn't grumble, complain or argue about his work for God. He won't selfishly murmur against his fellow man, but will live with the humility of Jesus. His outward conduct is "blameless" and his inner character is "pure," like unalloyed metal. There must be nothing impure in the heart that ought not to be there.

Our generation is very "crooked." People have minds, hearts and actions that are bent in all directions. It is also "depraved," i.e. "perverted, warped, and twisted. Christians are to shine like torchbearers in a sin-darkened world. We hold out the word of life to people in the same way as the host of a Greek banquet offered wine to his guests.

Paul encouraged the Philippians, for he wanted to be proud of them when Jesus returns to judge all our works of service. Paul didn't want to "run his race" or "labor" in the weight room of life for nothing! The Philippian Christians were trophies of a life invested for Christ. His life was poured out as a drink offering was poured on a meal offering or a burnt offering in the Old Testament (Genesis 35:14). (It was never added to a sin or trespass offering because they pictured Jesus' completed work of salvation). The drink offering went up in steam and disappeared. Only a humble person would want to be a "drink offering." Paul is now considering that he could die as a martyr very shortly.

Some believers are running in vain in the race of life. Their spiritual workouts are whimpy. No wonder they have little spiritual muscle. Are you "working out" the salvation God worked in you? What are you doing that is not in vain? Are you producing fruit for which will last when Jesus comes to judge your works? May God help us to work out in His power!

Read Philippians 2:19-30

Two Loyal Assistants

But you know that Timothy has proved himself, because as a son with his father he has served with me in the work of the gospel.

Philippians 2:22

LOYAL ASSISTANT COACHES are of great value in athletics. Good assistants take pressure off the head coach, deflect criticism, and make the team run more smoothly. Success depends to a great extent upon a good staff.

Paul had a small, but loyal staff of assistants encouraging him in prison. In fact, he felt a bit deserted by everyone but Timothy and Epaphroditis.

Timothy had no peers. Many others preferred their own ease and safety, desiring recognition instead of truth, holiness, and duty. Not Timothy. He stood out like a diamond in a world of self-serving people. Others did God's work only when it was to their advantage. Timothy genuinely put the cause of Jesus ahead of his own interests. He stood in contrast to one of Paul's former assistants, Demas, who deserted him (2 Timothy 4:10). Demas resembled many Americans — he loved this present world.

Epaphroditis ("charming") had brought money to Paul (4:18) and had come to encourage him. Paul calls him a "brother" (God was Father of both), a "fellow worker" (in God's workshop), and a "fellow soldier" in the conflict with evil. They were Christians "fighting side by side" (Gr. "systratioles") in spiritual warfare. Epaphroditis probably carried this letter to the Philippians. He had taken care ("served as priest") to Paul. He was loyal to Paul. He had been very ill and almost died, but Paul (who had the gift of healing) didn't or couldn't heal him. Nor is there evidence that his illness resulted from being out of God's will. In fact, he was serving God faithfully! Evidently his sickness was not the result of any specific sin. It resulted from serving Christ (v 30).

Epaphroditis was distressed, being far from home and knowing those in Philippi had heard of his illness. He risked ("paraboleuomai") his life in the service of Christ and devotion to Paul. The word "paraboleuomai" is a gambling term meaning he "gambled his life recklessly." God spared Paul wave upon wave of distressing circumstances by sparing Epaphroditis' life. Paul's loyal helper resembled the "Parabolani," men in Alexandria who nursed cases of plague and fever during epidemics.

It is interesting that Paul had some anxiety in his life. He who wrote, "Have no anxiety about anything" (4:6) wasn't perfect. We honor men like Paul and his friends, but they are not to be worshiped. Only God is great. Maybe Epaphroditis had not been honored back home (v 29). Even in churches today, sometimes the most committed Christians are not the most esteemed. To our shame, wealth and prestige often sway people more than the love of Jesus. But God knows the heart. He knows who is loyal — to Himself and to fellow believers. And He will graciously reward us some day!

Read Philippians 3:1-11

A Great Trade

But whatever was to my profit I now consider loss for the sake of Christ.

Philippians 3:7

THE WORLD CHAMPION YANKEES of 1998 made a great trade just prior to spring training of 1999. They sent popular and successful left-hander David Wells, who won 18 games and threw a no-hitter during their championship year, along with Homer Bush and Ghrame Loyd to the BlueJays for Roger Clemons, the best pitcher in baseball. It was a daring trade, one that brought speculation on both sides of the deal.

When Paul wrote about a daring trade he had made in Philippians 3, he seems to leave the theme of his preceding comments. "Finally" ("as for the rest"), he says, "Rejoice in the Lord." Being joyful in the Lord is a great command. We need this reminder constantly because it is so easy to become discouraged. Isn't it ironic that Paul, in prison, felt it necessary to remind free people in Philippi to rejoice in the Lord?

Paul warns us to beware of false teachers. He calls them "dogs," referring to the vicious scavengers of the area who ran wild, eating crumbs instead of feasting on healthy food. The term applies to Judaizers who taught that circumcising the flesh helped make them right with God instead of relying on the feast of God's grace. False teachers condemn people when they should teach of God's grace. They comfort people when they should be warning them of judgment. They were evil workers who gained influence in the body so they might destroy it. The sleeping American church today needs the warning of men like Paul.

False teachers followed Paul, questioning his credentials and his teaching that knowing Jesus is all one needs to be saved. They taught the religion of keeping Jewish laws to be right with God. Religious folks are occupied with beautiful buildings, elaborate ceremonies, traditions of men, or emotional buzzes. Paul had been the most religious of all, but he found it was worthless to be religious! He listed his religious credentials, then called them "rubbish" (dung)! As such, he flushed these credentials down the drain:

1. Circumcision — the basic rite of Judaism. Those circumcised may have good intentions, but the road to hell is paved with good intentions!

2. Israeli Nationality — Paul could trace his genealogy to Abraham. He was a "blue-blood" with religious credentials. This couldn't save him either.

3. Tribe of Benjamin — As a member of the choice group of the nation, Paul had prestige. But one's fraternity, society, or club affiliation cannot save!

4. Hebrew of Hebrews — Paul was a leader at the top of the heap, but he was lost.

5. Pharisee — He was a fundamentalist, believing Scripture, in angels, miracles, and the resurrection. Paul was nationalistic for God and country and he tried to establish God's kingdom on earth. This, too, did not save him.

6. Zealous for God — He had persecuted Christians and thought he was doing God a favor. Other Pharisees just ran the Christians out of town, but Paul hunted them down like rabbits. He hated Jesus and His followers — before he got saved!

7. Legalistic righteousness — He claimed to be "blameless" (not "sinless"). No one could fault Paul for not bringing the proper sacrifices to the temple. He was 100% Jewish. He performed all Jewish religious ritual. But it did not cleanse him from sin! He realized he was hopelessly lost (Romans 7:7).

One day, the risen Christ Jesus arrested Paul on the road to Damascus where he intended to persecute Christians! The seven things he had claimed as profit, he realized were worthless. Knowing Jesus, which had been of no value to him, was now all that mattered. He made a complete reversal in his "bookkeeping system." Christ became the only item on the credit side of the ledger and his religious credentials became manure! His own righteousness was as filthy rags (Isaiah 64:6). He lost everything to gain Christ, for he was disinherited by relatives, disowned by friends, and persecuted by Pharisees. Conversion radically changes everything and it continues to change everything! If there is no radical, lasting change in attitude and lifestyle, there is no conversion!

Salvation is by faith (v 9). We have nothing to bring to God. We are all unattractive sinners, condemned by our sin to eternal separation from God. But "in Christ" we are accepted by God and everything changes! Paul traded his efforts to be righteous for being placed "in Him." It was a better trade than the Yankees made for Roger Clemons! He got new purpose, new motivation, and a new lifestyle. He didn't sit in a rocking chair polishing his halo. Now his great ambition was to know Christ intimately. He wanted to know His power and share His sufferings. Perhaps he knew he would feel uncomfortable meeting those he had killed in heaven if he was now martyred! He doesn't say all must have this view of suffering and death, but he desired it. He chose a lonely road instead of comfort, luxury and ease. "Somehow" (martyred, death by old age, or the rapture), Paul knew he would be resurrected and see his Savior! All who are "in Christ" will see Him, too!

Read Philippians 3:12-4:1

Paul's Coaching Clinic

But one thing I do: Forgetting what is behind and straining toward what is ahead, I press on toward the goal to win the prize for which God has called me heavenward in Christ Jesus.
Philippians 3:13-14

DUKE BASKETBALL COACH Mike Krzyzewksi is a master motivator who puts on a "coaching clinic" by the way he handles his players. Once, when All-American Bobby Hurley had a four-game slump, he sat him down for a one-on-one taping session. Coach K showed Hurley a five-minute video of Bobby's pouting, whining, pointing fingers, and dropping his head.

"Bobby, is that the message you want to send your team-mates?" he asked quietly. From that moment on, Hurley became one of the country's best point guards.

Paul held a "coaches clinic" for Christians in the third chapter of Philippians. He told them, and us, to focus on one thing, to forget the past, and to strain forward to what is ahead. He certainly was a great coach in Christian living and his advice is relevant in the athletic world, too! Let's examine what he said.

First, Paul was single-minded. He had been saved for 30 years, but knew he had not reached the goal of knowing Christ as intimately as possible (v 10). He had not arrived and he was running hard to reach the goal of really knowing the Savior. He was not complacent or lazy. He was single-minded in his quest. "One thing I do," he said, not "100 things I dabble in." His purpose was to know Jesus and earn rewards in heaven. He pushed forward, straining as an Olympic runner for the finish line.

Second, Paul forgot the past, no matter how bad (murder of Christians) or how good (winning great numbers to Christ). He didn't mope over past, forgiven sins, nor did he dwell upon his achievements. Looking back leads to turning back and worry over the future saps one's strength. He pressed on daily to know Jesus. That was his purpose and direction.

Third, he told the Philippians to follow his example ("typos," "pattern" or "mold"). He was sure he had the mind of Christ on the matter of living daily, so he didn't shrink from being a "role model." He encouraged people to follow other good role models (v 17). Mature believers feel the same way. Others were content with lower goals (v 15), but God would clarify the truth to them. Living up to the truth we know is our great need (v 16).

Sadly, many professing Christians lived as *enemies* of Christ. With minds on earthly things, they were self-indulgent, worshiping their "bellies." This means they were gluttons concerning food or promiscuous sex. Like many today their chief concern was "where can we drink," "what can we eat," and "who can we sleep with." They lived lives of comfort and convenience, but they undermined the cause of Christ. They avoided thinking that their overeating, obesity, and sexual conquests related to their "Christianity." But they lived as enemies to everything Jesus represented. True Christianity means self-discipline. They took pride in their sins when they should have been ashamed. Paul said their destiny is destruction (Gr. "apoleia," eternal separation from God").

In contrast, Paul's citizenship was in heaven. Here on earth we merely live in a colony of believers, as the Philippians lived in a Roman colony. As the Roman soldiers of Philippi took pride in their citizenship and its privileges, we feel honored to be Jesus' representatives on earth. We eagerly await our Savior's return. Just as the greatest event in a Roman colony was the visit of the emperor, our greatest hope is the coming of Christ! By His resurrection power, He will transform us into His likeness! The Pharisees believed the flesh would be resurrected, but Paul taught our bodies would be transformed into a glorified body suited for heaven. Our lowly (not vile) bodies of scars, suffering, and sickness will be replaced by eternal health and youth! We can't wait for this to happen! It motivates us to heavenly living now!

The Philippian Christians were to Paul what the victory wreath meant to winners of the Greek races. They were his joy because he had won them to Christ, and his crown because he would be rewarded for it! He had both taught them and showed them how to stand for the Lord of Glory!

Read Philippians 4:2-9

Mental Attitude of a Winner

Rejoice in the Lord always! I will say it again: Rejoice!
Philippians 4:4

OLD-TIMER RUBE WADDELL ONCE BECAME a pouting pitcher as a result of a barbed comment from an opposing coach. As the Philadelphia ace took his last warm up pitch before facing St. Louis, the first base coach hollered, "Get out of here you big bum. You can't pitch."

Waddell looked at him with a wounded expression, dropped his glove on the mound, went to the outfield bleachers and sat among the crowd. Despite please from his manager and teammates, he stayed there all afternoon!

The Christian walk demands a mental toughness stronger than that which Rube Waddell demonstrated that day. Paul described it to the Philippians in Chapter Four. We are to "get along with each other, rejoice in the Lord, refrain from worry, and focus on the positive.

Even in the most vibrant Philippian church, two women had disrupted things by becoming contrary to each other. No details are given, but they were not acting in a Christ-like manner. The intervention of a third party was necessary to help them get along. No two people always agree, but believers must work together!

Paul says, "Rejoice in the Lord always." It is a matter of the will and demands mental toughness. If we refuse, we have no strength for living. To rejoice in Him is to enjoy His presence. Believers ought to be the most joyful, gentle, and considerate people. Jesus is with us and could return physically at any moment!

We are to refuse to worry about *anything*. To worry is to "be distracted" or "to have a divided mind." Instead, we must pray about everything, big and small, with thanksgiving. Prayer is talking with God. Petition is earnest pleading for heartfelt needs. We must turn worry into prayer and thank God immediately for His answers. He always answers with "Yes," "No," or "Wait." Don't pout when He says, "No," or "Wait!" Christians need mental toughness!

Fenelon, a mystic of the Middle Ages, said,

"Tell God all that is in your heart, as one unloads one's heart, its pleasures and its pains, to a dear friend. Tell Him your troubles, that He may comfort you; tell Him your joys, that He may sober them; tell Him your longings, that He may purify them; tell Him your dislikes, that He may help you to conquer them; talk to Him of your temptations, that He may shield you from them; show Him the wounds of your heart, that He may heal them; lay bare your indifference to good, your depraved tastes for evil, your instability. Tell Him how self-love makes you unjust to others, how vanity tempts you to be insincere, how pride disguises you to yourself as to others.

"If you pour out all your weaknesses, needs, troubles, there will be no lack of what to say. You will never exhaust the subject. It is continually being renewed. People who have no secrets from each other never want subjects of conversation. They do not weigh their words, for there is nothing to be held back;

neither do they seek for something to say. They talk out of the abundance of the heart, without consider-ation, just what they think. Blessed are they who attain to such familiar, unreserved intercourse with God."

When we resolve to pray with thanksgiving, the peace of God will guard ("phroureo," "set a watch with armed sentry" or "to keep securely locked") our hearts (emotions) and minds (thoughts). All believers have peace *with* God, which depends upon faith. But the peace *of* God depends upon prayer with thanksgiving. This inward tranquillity surpasses human reasoning. It is there when outward circumstances are terrible (Isaiah 26:3).

We can control our thoughts, but we must *want* to be pure! In verses 8-9, Paul lists elements of Greek moral phi-losophy. These verses also describe Jesus! We must think on whatever is true. This means thinking based upon the genu-ine and real, not upon the perceptions of men. We must think upon the honest (honorable, dignified), just (righteous) and pure. Jesus was pure, for Satan could not "hook onto" any sin in Him (John 14:30). We must think upon the lovely (gracious, agreeable, winsome), the admirable (positive, constructive), the excellent (that with mental, moral or physical superiority), and the praiseworthy. High thinking produces high living. Instead of sitting in church in a daze for an hour, contemplate the Lord Jesus. The peace of God will be yours in a very troubled world!

Read Philippians 4:10-23

Contentment

*. . . for I have learned to be content whatever the circum-
stances. I know what it is to be in need and I know what it is to
have plenty. I have learned the secret of being content in any
and every situation, whether well fed or hungry, whether living
in plenty or in want. I can do everything through him who gives
me strength.*

Philippians 4:11-13

THE ARMY OF ALEXANDER THE GREAT was marching on
Persia. At a critical point, it appeared that his troops would be
defeated. The soldiers had taken so much plunder from
previous campaigns that they had become weighted down and
were losing their effectiveness in combat. Alexander commanded that all spoils be burned. Some men complained
bitterly but soon came to see the wisdom of the order. A
historian wrote, "It was as if wings had been given to them —
they walked lightly again." Victory was assured.

Paul was a contented soldier in God's army. He had an
advanced degree from God's "School of Discipline!" When he
had nothing and was a prisoner, he didn't complain and
become discouraged. When he had plenty and was released
from prison, he didn't become greedy and proud. Over time
and difficult circumstances, Paul adjusted well to God's will.
He became a victor, not a victim. He wrote in 1 Timothy 6:6-
10 that "godliness with contentment is great gain." Contentment is greater than riches, for if a contented man is not rich
it doesn't matter because his lust for riches is removed!

Paul concluded that he could do all things *in* (not *through*)
the power of Christ. The "all things" carries the meaning of
everything within God's will. It implies he could endure trials
that came his way. God does not give us unlimited power to
do anything our selfish hearts desire. Our lives are like a
train, empowered by a powerful engine to run on rails. Trains
run through mountains, across deserts, and in rain, hail,
sleet and snow. The engine provides power as long as the
wheels stay on the tracks. But off the tracks, there is *no*

55

power! Likewise, the moment we depart from God's will through willful sin, rebellion against God's directives in Scripture, or lack of prayer — we become powerless.

Nevertheless, Paul thanked the Philippians for helping him financially. He had been run out of Philippi, had escaped out of Thessalonica (Acts 16-17), and had been supported only by the Philippian Christians. Their investment in Paul means they have a part to this day in getting God's Word to the world! Paul was glad that God would reward them and supply all their needs. This promise to supply needs (not wants) was made to those who gave sacrifically to God's work. He supplies our needs *according to* (in proportion to), not just "out of" His riches. It's all God's money and He gets all the glory (4:20).

The chains are still on Paul's wrists. He is still guarded by a Roman soldier. But he had won many in "Caesar's household" to Christ and his spirit is free! His mind is clean and his conscience is clear. He is a contented servant of Jesus. He hands this letter to Epaphroditis, who takes off for Philippi.

COLOSSIANS
Introduction

PAUL'S LETTERS TO CHRISTIANS while he was imprisoned in Rome (61-63 AD) make up the "Anatomy of the Gospel." His letter to the Ephesians emphasizes the church, the *body* of our Lord Jesus Christ, Paul wrote to Philemon about the *hands* (deeds) of a Christian slave named Onesimus. To the Philippians, Paul wrote about the *feet* with which we work out the gospel of Jesus. But to the Colossians, Paul wrote about the *Head* of the body, our Lord Jesus Christ!

Colosse was on a major trade route in Southern Phrygia, the adopted home of oriental mysticism. All sorts of ungodly ideas from the east pervaded the area. Paul wrote Colossians to combat the mixture of Jewish, Greek, Roman and mystical eastern ideas which diluted the Christian church, rendering it ineffective.

The first and chief heresy invading the Christian gospel was Gnosticism. Two basic errors made up this philosophy. One was that a higher knowledge beyond what God had revealed was available to only "enlightened ones." This led to an exclusive spirit. As McGee says, some people felt they had "knowledge in a jug and a stopper in their hands."

The second basic error of Gnosticism was that spirit is good and matter (the body) is evil. Therefore, the Gnostics denied the humanity of Jesus, saying He only "seemed" to have a body, that He did not really die and He wasn't raised bodily because He was only a "spirit-king." It was the high sounding ideas of man's religious spirit that kept man from God's Spirit and His grace. Satan had attacked Christianity through *religion,* hampering the true gospel of salvation by grace through the shed blood of Christ alone.

The church must remain focused on the Lord Jesus Christ and not on law, man's works, or religious tradition. All wisdom and knowledge are found in Him. Gnosticism encouraged worship through a series of mediating angels, and allegorically interpreted ancient writings for "enlightenment," the same false teachings as found in Buddhism, Hinduism and the New Age movement. These teachings do not mix with the gospel of

Christ. They come from hell and lead straight back to hell! Paul was making this clear as he wrote from prison to all believers down through the ages. May our wonderful Lord Jesus, who created the universe, walked upon this planet, died for our sins, and rose again bodily encourage you through this victorious book!

Read Colossians 1:1-2

The Will of the Head Coach

Paul, an apostle of Christ Jesus by the will of God . . .

Colossians 1:1

NO ATHLETE WILL BECOME as good as he can be without excellent coaching. But he must go beyond excellent coaching. The player must seek to know and do exactly what the coach desires if he is to be successful. Mere lip service is inadequate. The more a player trusts an outstanding coach, the more he reaches his potential.

Paul was an apostle by the will of God. He had found the will of his Head Coach and was doing it! Like any outstanding leader of men, God has a personal, directive will for those who follow Him. It is clearly possible to know God's will. That will concerned what Paul *was* — an apostle. What Paul *was* had implications for what Paul *did*. He spread the gospel of Jesus Christ to everyone.

Paul prayed for the "holy and faithful brothers in Christ at Colosse" (v 2). He asked that they "be filled with the *knowledge of His will* through all spiritual wisdom and understanding" (v 9). When the Colossians were so filled, it would greatly impact their lifestyles. God wants us to live lives worthy of Him, morally pure and above reproach. He wants us to please Him in everything we do and say. He desires that we produce good works, like a tree planted close to a river (Psalm 1).

Much of God's will is found in His Word. He promises to direct our paths if we trust and acknowledge Him as active in our lives. Solomon wrote, "Trust in the Lord with all your heart and lean not on your own understanding; in all your ways acknowledge him, and he will make your paths straight" (Proverbs 3:5-6).

He leads us in paths of righteousness for his name's sake (Psalm 23:3). He wants us to seek first His righteousness (Matthew 6:33). His will is more like a scroll than a blueprint. If an entire scroll is unrolled all at once, it gets all messed up. We couldn't comprehend the entire will of God very far ahead of time anyway. God reveals His will day by day as we seek and obey Him.

Yogi Bera said, "When you come to a fork in the road, take it." We laugh at Yogi and some of his lines, but how do we know which way to go in the decisions of life? Writers have illustrated finding God's will in various ways. Knofel Staton uses an umbrella to show that we are free to choose as long as our choices all fall under the umbrella of salvation, holiness, and a desire to please and serve Him. As we decide whom to marry, which job to take, and where to live, we are to use principles of God's Word, consider our gifts, use sanctified common sense, hear counsel of Godly Christians, and pray for wisdom. Bill Gothard says to make sure two "posts" line up as you sight down the fence row of life. One "post" is that which will be important ten years from now. The second "post" is that which will be important for eternity. He says that God gives us a vision (goal), allows the total destruction of that vision so we see we can never fulfill it ourselves, and then He brings it to pass. In this way, God (not man) is glorified! The Bible continually summons us to accept challenges beyond ourselves. We need not fear inadequacy — unless we are depending upon ourselves and not upon God!

Some people so lament their bad choices, thinking they have ruined God's will for them and must settle for "Plan B." This idea brings discouragement. But God is not in the business of using only those who have made all perfect decisions in the past. If this were the case, no one could qualify. He is in the forgiving business. He doesn't play spiritual "monopoly" with our lives ("Go directly to jail, do not pass go, do not collect $200"). Do you know anyone on Plan A? Many people of God are on Plan B, C, D, or Z! Our wonderful, almighty God is a God of the impossible and the miraculous! Praise His Holy Name!

59

Where the Bible speaks clearly, obey it. For example, Christians are told to never be unequally yoked with unbelievers (2 Corinthians 6:14). It is clear we should only marry or go into a business partnership with another committed Christian. But where Scripture is silent, we must totally give ourselves to God, listen to godly counselors who know us well, pray specifically and persistently, consider which doors are open, evaluate our talents and abilities, and then let God's peace dictate which choice to make. Colossians 3:15 says, "Let the peace of God rule in your hearts." This means God's peace "acts as an umpire" saying "yes" or "no," "go" or "stay." Without His peace, we must wait further upon Him. With His peace, we proceed with confidence.

We all come to forks in the road of life. We seek God's guidance to make choices. Having made a decision to take a certain path, we must not go part way along the road, stop and waste time in regret. We trust God that He led us to choose. Often, "no longer an option" is the sign over the other fork, and regret renders us powerless. Press on with confidence in Almighty God. We must never think we are out of God's will because of difficulties. Joseph was right in the middle of God's will while in prison. Paul and other heroes of the faith suffered greatly, but were right in the midst of God's will.

Finally, we need a role model as we seek the will of God. We have one: The Lord Jesus Christ. The attitude of Jesus Christ was always to do the will of His Father. Jesus said, "For I have come down from heaven not to do my will but to do the will of him who sent me" (John 6:38). If our attitude is like His, it becomes easier to make many of life's decisions. The mind set of doing God's will above our own is like the rails on a rain track. We have clear guidance on many issues. Jesus always did what pleased God the Father (John 8:29). He was always about His Father's business (Luke 2:49). He was troubled in the Garden of Gethsemane (John 12:27), yet He prayed, "Not my will, but yours be done" (Luke 22:42).Truly, Jesus came to model, to follow, and to do the will of the Father (Hebrews 10:7, 9). What a wonderful Savior!

Read Colossians 1:3-8

The Only Opinion that Counts

. . . . the word of truth, the gospel . . .

Colossians 1:5-6

UMPIRE BABE PINELLI once called Babe Ruth out on strikes, infuriating the great slugger. Reasoning fallaciously from raw numbers to moral weight, Ruth said, "There's 40,000 people here who know that last one was a ball, tomato head." Pinelli calmly replied, "Maybe so, but mine is the only opinion that counts."

Many people have their opinion about how to get to heaven, but the only opinion that counts is that of Almighty God! He has set the conditions for salvation and termed it the "gospel." The word "gospel" means "good news." Does God's gospel mean one must be born into a Christian family? Is the gospel only for white-skinned people? Or is it only for black-skinned folks? Is it for the rich or the poor? Can one be too evil to be saved? Are some people so good they needn't hear the gospel? Is one saved by being dunked under water? Or sprinkled with holy water? Does eating a piece of bread and drinking a sip of wine save a man? Or is it grape juice that does the trick?

The gospel is a simple message we are asked to believe in our hearts and to express with our words. We are asked to believe the gospel on the basis of certain facts. These include the following: Jesus Christ was the Son of God, born of a human virgin. He lived a perfect life and performed miracles. He was crucified for all our sins, was buried, and arose bodily to return to heaven. He has sent the Holy Spirit to represent Him in the world and in the lives of believers today. He is physically coming back to take all who believe in Him to be forever with Him!

We are asked to put our *faith* today in this gospel. Faith is not a leap into the dark, but a leap into the light of God's

61

gospel. Because of the presence of the Holy Spirit in us, we have *love* for other people. Love is the evidence that we have real faith in God. Christians will have real influence for God only when they love one another. We must love those of other churches, whether or not we agree with all their beliefs. We must love members of all races of people. The world only knows of our love for God by our love for others.

Finally, we have *hope* for the future. Faith rests in the past and love lives in the present, but hope looks toward the future. We anticipate the day we will see God in heaven. He will welcome us into His presence to enjoy endless fellowship with Him!

We are very rich people no matter what our material status today. Our sins are forgiven, our redemption is assured, our salvation is a present possession, God's Spirit and His nature indwell us, and the sure hope of Heaven is before us! We have no time for sin, Satan, or backsliding! What "good news" is this gospel of our Lord Jesus Christ!

Read Colossians 1:9-12

Spiritual Wisdom and Understanding

. . . we have not stopped praying for you and asking God to fill you with the knowledge of his will through all spiritual wisdom and understanding.

Colossians 1:9

FORMER SOCCER STAR Kyle Rote, Jr. showed much spiritual wisdom when he discussed the basis for his athletic success. "The presence of a living God and His unconditional love . . . set the stage for my athletic success because I then knew I could risk failure. My identity would not be based on whether I won or lost," he said.

What is spiritual wisdom? It involves discernment, perception, sound judgment, and insight based upon God's Word. Paul had a deep concern for the Colossians and he prayed constantly that they would know God's will through spiritual wisdom and understanding. How we need these same abilities today!

The Proverbs of Solomon reveal many benefits of wisdom, understanding, and discernment. He wrote, "My son, preserve sound judgment and discernment, do not let them out of your sight; they will be life for you, an ornament to grace your neck" (Proverbs 3:21-22). "Blessed is the man who finds wisdom, the man who gains understanding, for she is more profitable than silver and yields better returns than gold" (Proverbs 3:13-14).

We save ourselves much grief by applying spiritual wisdom and understanding. It is through such discernment we live lives worthy of the Lord and to pleasing to Him   (v 10). Sometimes it is hard to know which direction to move. We must listen to the voice of His Spirit. Jesus said, "He who belongs to God hears what God says" (John 8:47). But Satan and our own selfish minds speak, too. How do we know who is speaking? We use spiritual wisdom and discernment by studying God's Word and seeking His peace in every decision. Oliver Greene writes,

> "Most believers live a very shallow Christian life. To walk worthy of the Lord is to literally feel the bond of His redeeming blood; to feel the pain He suffered when He shed His blood for the remission of sins. To walk worthy of the Lord is to so love, cherish and worship Him that the very image of Himself is continually before us. To walk worthy of the Lord is to yield to His Spirit and to walk in such harmony *with* the Spirit that we will exhibit His purity, His piety, His humility, His love and His very life. We are to walk in His steps; we are to get into the yoke with Jesus and walk beside Him."

There is much religious chicanery on "Christian' television today. Lavishly dressed characters conduct spiritual "three-ring circuses," claim special revelation from God, promise immediate healing from every discomfort, and spread confusion via "laughing revivals." Some are frauds and are exposed, but only after undiscerning viewers have sent them millions of dollars of God's money. Only spiritual wisdom and discernment enables us to distinguish truth from the error so subtly mixed into their teachings.

It is through spiritual wisdom that we are strengthened with His power (v 11). This power comes not from ourselves, but from God! It is not "prayed down," "worked up," or "acquired in a seminary". It is available to all believers who keep their eyes upon Jesus and place their hope and faith in Him. It is through His power, given us to resist evil, conquer fear, banish doubt, take advantage of opportunities, and overcome all difficulties that we "bear fruit" in every good work (v 10). Christians cannot help but bear fruit of love, joy, peace and other virtues because they are living branches attached to the true vine, Jesus Christ. "But the fruit of the Spirit is love, joy, peace, patience, kindness, goodness, faithfulness, gentleness, and self-control" (Galatians 5:22-23).

It is through spiritual wisdom that we grow in our knowledge of God. By discerning His ways we grow in experiential knowledge of Him. We will never know everything about His wonderful nature. No one can explain the Trinity adequately. But we can discover some of His ways and His plans for us. The more we know Him, the more confidence we have in Him. We will lean upon Him for support, confide in Him when we have problems, and enjoy being His child.

Through spiritual wisdom we have great endurance and patience (v 11). We give thanks to God continually (v 12), for He has saved us from sin and promised eternal life! He has qualified us to share in the inheritance of the saints in His kingdom of light! Who are the saints? Does some church make saints of dead martyrs? Do they play football in New Orleans? No! All who belong to Jesus by faith in His shed blood are "saints" according to God's Word! We have a wonderful future with Him because of His victory on the cross! Praise His Holy Name!

Read Colossians 1:13

Two Kingdoms at War

For he has rescued us from the dominion of darkness and brought us into the kingdom of the son he loves . . .

Colossians 1:13

NFL SAFETY WILLIAM WHITE has described two opposing kingdoms and the end result of following each. "We have a choice of two game plans in life: God's way or man's way," he said. "God's way leads to victory and man's way leads to death."

There are really only two kingdoms in existence. All men are part of one, never part of two at the same time. There is the dominion of darkness. The Bible says that the god of this age (Satan) has blinded the minds of unbelievers so that they cannot see the light of the gospel of the glory of Christ, who is the image of God (2 Corinthians 4:4). The dominion of darkness tells men that:

1. Seeing is believing.
2. Save your life above all else.
3. Claim recognition for self.
4. Lord it over others.
5. Exalt yourself.
6. Look out for #1.
7. Get all you can.
8. Love comes and goes — it is a feeling.
9. Hate enemies and get revenge.
10. Cover up your mistakes.
11. Pull yourself up by your own boot straps.
12. Seek pleasure — eat, drink, be merry (tomorrow we die anyway).
13. Better check out your horoscope.
14. Scripture is outdated and old-fashioned.
15. Jesus was only a wise teacher who died as a martyr.

65

The other kingdom is the kingdom of God. In Colossians 1:13 it is called the "kingdom of the Son he loves." Jesus said, "My kingdom is not of this world" (John 18:36). His kingdom is invisible now, but soon Jesus will appear and the kingdom of this world will become the kingdom of our Lord and of His Christ, and He will reign forever and ever" (Revelation 11:15). Satan will be bound in the abyss (Revelation 20:3). The principles of God's kingdom include:

1. Believing God when you cannot see Him (John 20:29).
2. Give your life (Matthew 16:25).
3. Seek no recognition (Matthew 6:1-6).
4. Be a servant of others (Mark 9:35; 10:42-45).
5. Humble yourself (Luke 14:11).
6. Look out for other's interests (Philippians 2:3-4).
7. Give all you can (Luke 6:38).
8. Love unconditionally — it is a matter of the will (John 13:34).
9. Love your enemies and forgive (Matthew 5:44; Colossians 3:13).
10. Confess your sins (1 John 1:9).
11. Not by might, nor by power, but by my Spirit (Zechariah 4:6)
12. We will appear before Christ for judgment (2 Corinthians 5:10).
13. Search the Scriptures (John 5:39).
14. Scripture is inspired by God and eternal (2 Timothy 3:16; Matthew 24:35).
15. Jesus is the Lord; He arose from the dead, will return to earth, and all will bow before Him (Romans 14:9-12).

Man cannot build the kingdom of God. God is the One who builds His kingdom and He does it one person at a time. The moment a man, woman, or child trusts Jesus Christ as Savior, that person is "rescued from the dominion of darkness and brought into the kingdom of the Son." Paul says God "has rescued" Christians (past tense). Though we will inherit the glorious benefits of heaven later, we have already been rescued from Satan's dominion and been placed into God's kingdom under King Jesus! Peter wrote, "But you are a chosen people, a royal priesthood, a holy nation, a people belonging to God, that you may declare the praises of him who called you out of darkness into his wonderful light" (1 Peter 2:9).

Before we trusted Christ we were living in ignorance and blindness. Archibald Hunter says, "We were under a realm of sinister superhuman forces menacing our lives." We *could* not see because we *would* not see (believe) the truth. But the Son of Man came to seek and to save lost humanity (Luke 19:10). He chose us, making us a royal priesthood to intercede for others. We are now a holy nation of believers who belong to God. How wonderful to have escaped Satan's dark kingdom! How great to be placed into God's kingdom with our sins forgiven, redeemed by the blood of His cross! We are part of His permanent kingdom. Today we don't see its full manifestation. But it is no less real. When Jesus returns, we will reign with Him over the entire world! Hallelujah!

Read Colossians 1:14

Redemption

. . . in whom we have redemption, the forgiveness of sins.
Colossians 1:14

THE ANCIENT SLAVE TRADE was big business. It seems hard to imagine, but at one time 70 percent of the population in the Roman empire was enslaved! Slaves were bought, sold, and traded in markets as active as America's Wall Street today. Occasionally, a benevolent owner would purchase a slave in the market and actually set him free! Several words translated "redemption" in the New Testament describe this magnanimous deed.

"Redemption" is exactly what God has done for man with the death of Jesus Christ on the cross. Jesus paid for our liberation from sin with the very idea of setting us free! Redemption means our sins are forgiven. For all who take sin seriously (and God does!) this is an absolutely overwhelming truth. Ephesians 1:7 says our redemption is through His blood. When Jesus said, "It is finished" (John 19:30) while dying on the cross, He meant that the price had been paid in full for our redemption. No further price is required! Mark 10:45 says He came to give His life as a ransom for many.

Words can't express the significance of the price Jesus paid to free us from slavery to sin and death. Every little sin (if there were such a thing) and every big sin (it makes no difference) are paid for only by the blood of Jesus. But all sins are totally removed by His powerful blood!

His redemption is instantaneous. It is not a process. To apply it to our lives, we simply believe, receive it, and we are free from the slavery of our sin. God will not force us to believe Him, but what person in his right mind would prefer slavery to the glorious freedom He offers?

Read Colossians 1:15-20

Jesus: Who Is He?

He is the image of the invisible God, the firstborn over all creation.

Colossians 1:15

TO SPORTS FANS, the names of Michael Jordan, Troy Aikman, and Ken Griffey, Jr. are defined by what these great athletes do. Michael Jordan was one of basketball's all-time greats and was known for his leaping ability. Troy Aikman is recognized as a great leader of Super Bowl Champions and Ken Griffey, Jr. has set a standard of excellence as a major league hitter. What these men have done gives them great identity with fans.

The name Jesus Christ, however, rises far above any athletic hero because of *who He is,* as well as *what He has done!* In five short verses, Paul describes the person of Christ in answer to the heresies of Gnosticism (which said Jesus had no physical body) and Arianism (which said Jesus was a created being). This section answers all false cults (including Mormonism, Jehovah's Witnesses, Unitarianism) which teach false doctrine about the Savior.

Jesus Christ is the *image* of the invisible God. He is the exact likeness, the personal representative of God the Father. He doesn't just resemble God, but He manifests all God is to us! The invisible God is now visible! He became audible, approachable, knowable, and personally available to us! While we may *reflect* God's glory, Jesus *is* the glory of God! He said, "Anyone who has seen me has seen the Father" (John 14:9).

Jesus Christ is the firstborn over all creation. He is not "first-created," for He always existed. "Firstborn" indicates His priority in rights and position over His creation. He existed before creation and He is eternally sovereign Lord *and* heir of all things.

Jesus Christ is Creator of everything. Our small galaxy (The Milky Way) is a flat disk with a bulge in the center. It is 100,000 light years across, 10,000 light years thick and made up of 100 billion stars — earth being one of them. Why did God create everything? He knew He would have to redeem humanity by the cross. Why take the trouble? If God had remained alone, He would have been no less God. But alone, no one would see Him, praise Him, and worship Him for who He is! He created everything for His praise and glory, to display Himself in creatures holy and blameless. He wanted all creation to share His happiness and blessedness.

Jesus Christ is pre-eminent over all things. He is the great "I Am" of the Old Testament (John 8:58). He is the Center of the universe. Man, man's problems, angels, or earth's riches are not the center. When we center all our attention upon Him, we get back to reality!

Jesus Christ holds all things together. He sustains all things. He maintains the orbits of each planet, the coming of day and night, and the life of every living creature. He maintains order and harmony in His universe. He holds every atom together and when He allows one to be split the explosion is devastating! Without His sustaining power, everything would disintegrate. Thanks to Jesus, we live in a cosmos, not a chaos.

Jesus Christ is head of His church. He is "Boss" (Lord) over all believers who make up His body. He is the Source of life, the controlling Head, the guiding Governor. The true church is a living organism through which He carries out His purpose on earth.

Jesus Christ is the beginning, the firstborn from among the dead. He is the first and only one to rise from the dead by His own power. Because God raised Him, He can raise us! Through His resurrection, He abolished death for all who believe.

Jesus Christ is supreme over everything. His is an unshared supremacy. He is in a class by Himself. It isn't enough to recognize Him as present or even prominent — He is "pre-eminent!"

All the fullness of God dwells in Jesus Christ. The Gnostics described about forty descending levels of angelic beings ("aeons"), which in total made up God. Paul wrote, "For in Christ all the fullness of the Deity lives in bodily form" (Colossians 2:9). He has all power and authority. There is no other manifestation of God.

Jesus Christ is the Reconciler of all things. Only God could create all things, head the church, and reconcile all things to Himself. Man had left God and needed to be brought back. Jesus brought us back by the blood of His cross!

If we want to see the true picture of Jesus, our picture must be enlarged! He is bigger than Jordan, Aikman, or Griffey, Jr. What He has done makes their achievements seem so small. Who He is overwhelms us!

Read Colossians 1:21-23

Reconciliation

Once you were alienated from God and were enemies in your minds because of your evil behavior. But now he has reconciled you by Christ's physical body through death to present you holy in his sight, without blemish and free from accusation.
Colossians 1:21-22

STEVE LARGENT WAS A GREAT NFL receiver before leaving football to become an Oklahoma congressman. Largent is never bashful about the most important things in life. "Real satisfaction can only be found in a personal relationship with

God through His Son, Jesus Christ, who became, and still is, the greatest expression of God's goodwill toward us," he says.

Steve Largent did not always feel this way. At one time, Steve, like everyone of us, was alienated from God. He was in need of a Savior to reconcile him to God. It's not only the pagans in the jungle who are alienated from God. All people — black and white, rich and poor, Americans, Africans and Asians — who have never trusted Christ to save them are alienated from a Holy God. We are not naturally good people. We are sinners under a curse, estranged from God as shown by our evil behavior. Naturally we had a hostile attitude toward God, a mental antagonism like many "intellectuals" who reject Christ's blood sacrifice on their behalf. As the old Niké commercial said, "We did bad things, man." The fact that we are not basically good is self-evident, but it is very hard for Americans to accept. Nevertheless, it is true.

But now, all believers in Jesus are reconciled to God. This means the enmity between God and us has been removed. We are brought near to Him. Formerly enemies, we are now friends of God! How were we reconciled? We were reconciled by Christ's physical body through death. Jesus had a real body, suffered real pain, and physically died. He was God in a human body. Without flesh there could be no death. Without His death, we could never be reconciled to God from our sin and separation. But He died for us! This was totally *God's* idea. No man sat down and dreamed up the method of reconciliation. Could you imagine a man, in trying to figure out how to be justified before God in spite of his own sin saying, "I know what you should do, God. You take on a human body (by supernaturally making Mary pregnant), be born (so as to be 100% God and 100% man without a sinful nature), live 33 years (do miraculous signs and wonders), let us mock, torture and crucify you, and then rise in three days for our justification." No man would devise such a plan. Man's efforts are toward self-justification, trying to *do* something to make himself feel worthy of acceptance by God. All religions attempt to "pull man up by his own bootstraps," which is impossible. Christianity is not a religion, but it is God doing the work and getting the glory. It is all His idea.

Romans 5:8 says, "But God demonstrates his own love for us in this: While we were still sinners, Christ died for us." Paul adds in 2 Corinthians 5:18-20, "All this is from God, who reconciled us to himself through Christ and gave us the ministry of reconciliation: that God was reconciling the world to himself in Christ, not counting men's sins against them. And he has committed to us the message of reconciliation. We are therefore Christ's ambassadors, as though God were making his appeal through us. We implore you on Christ's behalf: Be reconciled to God."

There is no reason in God's mind for you to stay separated from Him! Because of Christ's death for you, God will accept you! The problem is in your mind. It is up to you to be reconciled to God by coming through the "gate" He has provided: Jesus Christ. He is the "door" (John 10:9/KJV). He is the "way" (John 14:6). And He is the *only* way ever devised by God by which you may come. Acts 4:12 says, "There is no other name under heaven given among men by which you *must* be saved!"

Verse 23 says that Jesus will present us holy (set apart), without blemish, and free from accusation (of Satan and ungodly people) if (since) we continue in faith. We cannot present ourselves as such, but He can and He will! No one will dare accuse us before Him — for He has justified us! Paul uses the "if" of argument, not the "if" of condition in this verse. In our language, we would say, "If you are a child of God, you will continue in the faith, established and firm."

The gospel extends great hope to us. It is our *only* hope! What is the gospel? It is not that Jesus was a kind of "Spirit-Being" who didn't really die and therefore couldn't be raised from the dead, as false teachers (Gnostics) were teaching in Colosse. The gospel, of which Paul was a servant, is that Jesus died for our sins, was buried, was raised on the third day and appeared in bodily form to hundreds of people (1 Corinthians 15:3-8). He really lived, died, arose from the dead, and will return for us. He reconciled us to God! Hallelujah! What a Savior!

Read Colossians 1:24-29

The Body of Christ

. . . for the sake of his body, which is the church.

Colossians 1:24

THERE IS A CITY along the Texas coastline that has one of the greatest names of any city ever built. Founded many years ago by Christians, it was named Corpus Christi, "the body of Christ." It is one more example of the Christian heritage of the United States of America.

Every person, black or white, rich or poor, male or female, who has trusted Jesus Christ alone for salvation from sin has been made part of His body. We have all been baptized by the Holy Spirit into His body (1 Corinthians 12:13). We are part of Him! This "mystery," or "truth long hidden but now revealed," is a great reason for joy in our hearts (Ephesians 3).

The devil and sinful men hate Jesus Christ, the Head of the body. The only way Satan can hurt Jesus today is to persecute those making up His body on earth. Paul said that the sufferings of Christ overflow into our lives (2 Corinthians 1:5). We sometimes suffer because of our oneness with Him. This Christ rejecting world will see that we suffer in some form if we stand for Him. Paul's suffering (and ours) added nothing to the finished redemptive suffering of Jesus. It occurs as a *result* of our salvation. *Everyone* who lives a Godly life in Christ Jesus suffers for it in this world (2 Timothy 3:12). Just as in the physical body we feel pain in our head when any part suffers, Jesus feels every heartache, bump and bruise that we receive. In this sense, we "fill up what is lacking in His sufferings."

Paul worked hard to proclaim Jesus as Head of the body. He didn't preach a religion, a system of rules, or a code of ethics. He saw everyone as a potential part of Christ's body (1:28). He didn't shun people who disagreed with him, but he reached out to try to win them to Christ and present them complete in Christ. Paul admonished ("counseled") and taught ("instructed") everyone so we might mature and be unhindered by the false teaching of the Gnostics.

73

The Head makes all the decisions for the good of the body. Every desire and craving of the body is subject to the Head. We have a wonderful Head. He governs in love, based on purpose and principle. Our knowledge is limited to our body parts and sometimes we don't even know ourselves! We never know ourselves as well as He knows us. So we receive great comfort from His directions. After all, we are led by a living Head, the Great Sovereign Lord of the Universe!

As Jesus' hands and feet, eyes and ears, how intensely are you serving Him? Do you hear His wise directions and respond quickly and obediently? Or do you respond spasmodically or not at all? Our Head desires and deserves quick and complete response to His every directive!

Read Colossians 2:1-8

Christ: God's Mystery

See to it that no one takes you captive through hollow and deceptive philosophy, which depends on human tradition and the basic principles of this world rather than on Christ.
Colossians 2:8

PAUL WOULD HAVE MADE a great coach. He was a fine instructor of fundamentals. He was a great encourager. And he persisted in the race of life with great intensity. In Colossions 2:1, he writes that he struggled ("agona"), like an athlete in a contest, on behalf of Christians who were being threatened by man's false teachings.

Jesus Christ is the "mystery of God." A mystery is something previously hidden but now revealed. In the Old Testament, it was not revealed that Jesus would personally come to indwell both Jews and Gentiles, making all who believe in Him His special people. God is now knowable and personal! When man receives Jesus, he receives a person and not merely a high-sounding philosophy. Paul was not against true philosophy ("love of wisdom"), for he was a scholar, very scientific in his thinking. But the false philosophies of the world left Christ out. When man refuses God's *revelation* of

Christ and substitutes his own ideas, traditions, and philosophies, he is in great danger.

Satan's first desire is to see us burn in hell with him. But he has forever lost all believers in Jesus! Still, he doesn't give up trying to influence us through false teachers who would steal our power, joy and influence for Christ in the world.

We must believe the correct doctrine of Christ. This includes His virgin birth, the fact that He is fully God and fully man, His blood atonement for our sins, His miracles and His death, His resurrection and His return to rule this world. Many deceivers ("false religious teachers") are in the world (2 John 7-11). Anyone who doesn't believe and teach these basic truths about Jesus is an antichrist and should be avoided if he calls himself a "Christian." Any compromise on these basics results in loss of power, joy, and influence for Christ to others.

Paul's goal for those he taught was that we know Jesus, the "mystery of God." *He* is the answer to life's questions. Man's hollow philosophy is not the answer. None of the world's esteemed philosophers (Plato, Kant, Locke, Sarte, Bultman, etc.) have a high view of God's Word. They use human wisdom to seek answers to the problems of life. J. Vernon McGee said that is similar to "a blind man looking in a dark room for a black cat that isn't there!" There is no hope of finding truth via man's wisdom. Truth is found by the *revelation* of God in Christ. Sarte's conclusions result in suicide, deceptive New Age teachings leave people lost and unfulfilled, and the lie of atheistic evolution brings feelings of great worthlessness and lack of purpose.

Likewise, the hollow sham of human tradition is no solid basis for finding meaning in life. It is poor policy to believe anything because a relative or church leader of the past believed it. It is Jesus Christ — not any church — who is infallible. Church structure and alleged mystic appearances of Mary or others can be unreliable and deceptive. Visions and non-biblical revelations are not authoritative.

Paul was concerned that we be "kidnapped" by these "illusions" and seduced from simple faith in Christ. Legalism holds people in spiritual slavery and asceticism, with its harsh treatment of the body, fails to make us more spiritual. Jesus Christ is not a philosophy, but a *Person!* He is the answer to the problems of life. How simple — yet how profound!

Read Colossians 2:9-15

Victory Snatched from Defeat

And having disarmed the powers and authorities, he made a public spectacle of them, triumphing over them by the cross.
Colossians 1:15

FORMER DALLAS COWBOY QUARTERBACK Roger Staubuch led his team to many great comebacks on the football field. In the face of seemingly hopeless odds, Roger somehow got his team into the end zone for the winning score. "Every time I stepped on the field, I believed my team was going to walk off the winner, somehow, some way," he said.

All appeared lost when Jesus was nailed to the cross, suffered horribly for six hours, and died a criminal's death. But three days later He arose from the dead, snatching victory over sin, death, and the grave from the very jaws of defeat. It was a comeback that makes any football victory pale in comparison!

It required the supernatural power of God to raise Jesus from the dead. The fact that the grave could not keep Him proved His divinity and His power. All the glory of God the Father, all His power, and all His attributes are found in Christ. Deity is not distributed up and down a whole series of forty angels (aeons) as the Gnostics taught. All of Deity is found in Christ! Because our minds are finite, this is beyond our understanding. But it is not beyond our belief! God created everything by His Word (Jesus), prepared a body for His Word (John 1:1,14), and experienced death for every man through that body.

Because Jesus dwells within all believers, we are completely fulfilled in Him. The word "complete" is a nautical term meaning we are "ready for the voyage" of life. We need no additional plan of salvation or source of grace. Fulfillment comes only by being "in Christ." Apart from Him, man finds only emptiness. The atheistic philosopher Jean Paul Sarte said, "Life is an empty bubble on the sea of nothingness." No wonder he lived in futility and self-destruction. He refused the fullness of God in Christ!

The Old Testament Jews identified outwardly with God by circumcision. Today, it is not circumcision of the body but spiritual circumcision of the heart that is important. Any person of any nationality can identify with God by allowing Him to "circumcise" their heart. This is not a ritual, but it is *symbolized* by water baptism, which denotes death to sin and resurrection to a new life. It also pictures the baptism of the Spirit of God, which occurs the moment a person believes in Jesus (1 Corinthians 12:13). It is important to note that we are saved by faith, not by the ritual of being dunked or sprinkled with water. Without saving faith, water baptism is an empty, meaningless ceremony. Sadly, many people go through the religious ritual of baptism, but never put their faith in Christ alone to save them.

We were "snatched" from the jaws of defeat by the Lord Jesus when He died and arose again! We owed a great debt to a holy God who gave us His righteous law. Because we could not and did not keep God's law, Jesus nailed this "debt certificate" to the cross and declared it "paid in full." The condemning power of the law was nailed there with Him! God has saved us, raised us to a new life, and joined us to His Son! Why return to an absolute legalistic set of rules we couldn't keep in the first place? We have a new nature led by God's Spirit which we can now follow! His standard of love for others is higher than any law.

The devil and his demons railed against God and against us. Jesus disarmed them and made a public display of these evil powers! After brutal warfare on the battlefield of life, Jesus stripped the armor from His fallen foe as a triumphant Roman general would strip his enemies and lead them behind his chariot through the streets of his home city. Jesus did this to Satan! He made a public spectacle of the evil one! We are completely delivered from the evil powers which had defeated us. Praise to our glorious King!

Read Colossians 2:16-23

Religion vs Relationship

These are a shadow of the things that were to come: the reality, however is found in Christ.

Colossians 2:17

PRO GOLFER SCOTT SIMPSON knows the difference between the shallow things of this world and a real relationship with Jesus. "My contentment isn't based on where I stand on the money list. It isn't based on performance. It is just based on Jesus Christ and having a right relationship with Him," he said.

Colossians 2:16 begins with a "therefore." Whenever this word appears in Scripture, it's a good idea to find out what it is *there for.* "Therefore" connects the preceding thought — that God has given us life in Christ, canceled the condemning power of the law by nailing it to the cross, and disarmed all accusing powers and authorities (demons or religious men) — with what is to follow. And what follows? What follows is Paul's teaching that we are not to submit to any list of man-made "dos" and "don'ts." Paul lists legalistic rules, rituals, seasons, and ceremonies. These make up men's version of religious observances as a substitute for Christianity. Every day and ever week is holy unto the Lord. Real Christianity is daily and free, not chained to rites and seasons.

External rituals are a shadow of the real thing. A relationship with Christ is the real substance. All Old Testament religious observances pointed to the Lord Jesus, and now that He has come we must look to Him. Believers belong to a body (of Christ), not to a system. We are part of an organism, not an organization. Legalistic teaching that we must obey rituals and laws in the Old Testament comes from demons (1 Timothy 4:1-14). We are to let no man "disqualify" us for the prize (v 18). The word means to "act as an umpire" to deny our claim to rewards for faithful service. We have direct access to God through Christ and need not go through angels, as the false teachers (Gnostics) advocated. These Gnostics professed to be extremely knowledgeable. They were highly educated and proud of it. They taught that Jesus was of a highest order of spirits, not God in the flesh. They gave angels a part in obtaining our salvation. (At one time, the angel Gabriel was worhiped at Colosse.) Paul warned against their false humility and the lying precepts which would entangle Christians. He proclaimed Jesus as Head of His body, the church (v 19). They rejected Jesus as God in the flesh.

Paul says, "We died with Christ . . ." (v 20). Death means separation. We are separated from dead religion since we are identified with Christ's death for us! What is religion? It is man doing works to make himself acceptable to God and to gain credit. Christianity is God working through men and God getting the credit. In religion, man creates God in his own image (imagination) and searches for such a one (Buddhism, Hinduism, etc.). The True God created man in His image and sought us by becoming man in Christ.

Many religious groups stress certain don'ts: "touch not, taste not, handle not" (v 21). The Christian is free from these rules of men. Nor is the false humility of neglecting or torturing the body of any value. These things make man feel religious, but they don't control fleshly devices at all. Man's idea is to perfect his own character by keeping rules. But doing so only inflates his own proud religiosity. The reality of a relationship with God is found in Christ (v 17). Religion, on the other hand produces only a false humility (v 18). Religion is a poor substitute for a relationship with Jesus Christ.

Read Colossians 3:1-4

The Heart and Mind of a Winner

Set your minds on things above, not on earthly things. For you died, and your life is now hidden with Christ in God.

Colossians 3:2-3

EVERY COACH IS THANKFUL to have athletes with tremendous desires to win. They use many phrases to describe the heart and mind-set needed for victory on the athletic field. "Winners never quit, quitters never win," "Champions make every second count," and "There is no 'I' in 'team'" are slogans which motivate players to succeed. Each of their phrases are concerned with the athlete's mental and emotional focus.

The mental and emotional focus of a champion in Christ is as easy to identify as that of an athletic champion. The h*eart* of a believer who runs the race of life to win is set upon heavenly things. After all, our head coach (Jesus Christ), our home and our treasures are all in heaven. Our affections must be there, too. Our attachment does not belong to trophies, rings, money, or prestige. Our hearts must not even be set upon any church or teacher, but upon Jesus alone.

Though we should not despise the good things on earth and may win championships or become wealthy, our hearts are not to be set upon earth's rewards or pleasures. After all, what honor given by man is better than God's promises that we are seated with Jesus in His presence? Which of man's awards matches the crowns He will give for faithfulness to Him? What power on earth approaches the power of the Holy Spirit who lives in us? What fame matches being a son of Almighty God? What riches compare with our wealth in heaven as a joint heir with Jesus? What earthly pleasure remotely compares with those found at His right hand? NONE!

The mind of a champion who runs to win is also set upon things in heaven. Such a winner sees events in light of eternity, so his world view differs from those of folks who seek only earthly things. When believers in Jesus hear of tragedy, we pray to the God who is in control. If a believer loses everything, he rejoices that he can never lose the things that count eternally! As evil intensifies and men faint from fear, we know God has the last word and He says Jesus will reign on earth! We know who wins and we will win with Him!

Sheep eat grass. Pigs eat and wallow in slop. It is in their nature to live this way. Real believers love Jesus and feed upon God's Word. Unbelievers wallow in sin and enjoy it. It's natural for believers to enjoy praising God and for unbelievers to commit sexual sins, get drunk, and serve selfish egos. But a believer in Jesus has died with Christ and been raised to a new life. He is not attracted to the "slop" of this world.

When Jesus was nailed to the cross, the law we could not keep, the debt we could not pay, and our old nature was nailed there with Him. Today, we live by faith in Christ (not law), our debt is fully paid, and our love for Jesus dictates our deeds. We are identified with Him in death and resurrection. It will be our glory to be with Him when He reappears. It is to His glory that He claims us!

Read Colossians 3:5-10

Our Old Evil Nature

Put to death, therefore, whatever belongs to your earthly nature: sexual immorality, impurity, lust, evil desires, and greed, which is idolatry.

Colossians 3:5

THE BEAUTY OF A FRESHLY GROOMED major league ballpark, the pure white clean uniforms of each player, and the rows of cheering fans sometimes make one feel that all is right with those who play the game. But then we consider the selfish temper tantrums, the sexual crimes, and the money grabbing contract disputes, and we are reminded of the old, evil nature indwelling even the brightest of today's stars. It is this nature that repels fans and brings disrepute to the game.

All of us possess this evil nature. The apostle Paul tells us how to handle it. Like coin, his writing always has two sides. The doctrinal side is we died in principle when we accepted Jesus' death for us. The practical side is we put to death all the drives of our evil nature.

It is unpopular to teach that mankind is an ugly brood of sinners. But it is God's truth. Romans 3:23 says, "For all have sinned and fall short of the glory of God." People want to believe we are basically good folks. Even after two world wars and the mass extinction of our own kind, we prefer to believe Ann Frank's line from her diary, "In spite of everything, I still believe people are really good at heart." But nothing could be further from the truth! The Bible and our own experience teaches that we are sinners in need of a drastic change at the core of our beings. Only when Jesus enters our lives are we changed.

Paul lists several acts and attitudes belonging to our earthly nature, including sexual immorality, impurity, lust and evil desires. Americans wallow in these sins. Our TV sets constantly reinforce our impure thoughts and deeds with degrading words and scenes. People watch this trash because it relates so closely to their evil natures. But Christians are to put that nature to death in a practical way and not to *feed* it! Lack of nourishment and exercise will kill these evil habit patterns.

Lust leads to sin and sin always pays off in death. No one has ever gotten away with disobeying God's laws. Romans 6:23 states, "For the wages of sin is death." Death may come via AIDS, drug overdose, drunken driving or it may take years of evil behavior — but it is certain. We are to avoid sin by counting our old nature crucified with Christ.

Paul ends this list of evil with "greed, which is idolatry." The Greek word used means "ruthless and aggressive self-seeking." This passion to have more becomes idolatry because *gain* becomes god! What a man strongly desires to own actually owns part of him! God says to have no gods before Him!

Paul's second list of evil attitudes must be taken off like a dirty shirt. The first is anger, which doesn't contribute to righteousness. It is right to be angry at sin, but we often get angry at the wrong things. Rage is a fierce outburst of uncontrolled wrath. We must be rid of wrath. Malice is a vicious desire to spitefully injure others. It includes ill will which rejoices in evil done to others. Slander is evil talk about others, including reckless insults. Filthy language includes all swearing and unclean stories. We must stop all lying. There are no little, white lies. All lies are big and black and one of a child's first sins is to lie. Lying is Satan's native language. "When he (Satan) lies, he speaks his native language, for he is a liar and the father of lies" (John 8:44).

Christians have had this old nature crucified with its passions and desires (Galatians 5:24). God does it for us. He nailed our sins and our evil nature to the cross with Jesus. Now He expects us to act accordingly, by counting it a "done deal." From the moment we accept Christ, the new nature of Jesus wages war against the old, evil nature. We must win the battle in daily practice, or the old self makes life miserable! Thank God, the battle is won by the indwelling Holy Spirit's control!

Read Colossians 3:10-17

Our New Nature

. . . and have put on the new self, which is being renewed in knowledge in the image of its Creator.

Colossians 3:10

THOUGH WOODY HAYES had his faults, he was acknowledged as a great college football coach. Woody was a strict disciplinarian at Ohio State and he led the Buckeyes to numerous Big Ten and Rose Bowl titles. Though he had rules, he knew rules were insufficient to get the most from each player. "We control by attitudes — positive mental attitudes — not by rules," he believed.

The old nature of man makes rules necessary. But it is the God-given new nature, that changes a life from the inside, allowing a person to fulfill his potential, and to please Him. Originally God made us in His image. We marred that image by sinning. Now that image is renewed by the knowledge of God! Christians are to "put on the new self." Our regenerated, spiritual nature, which is in tune with God, is to manifest God to others. Ephesians 4:23-24 says, ". . . to be made new in the attitude of your minds; and to put on the new self, created to be like God in true righteousness and holiness."

We know God by the Holy Spirit He has given us. The Spirit regenerates our spiritual nature and teaches us about Him. The old, natural man is ignorant of God and is spiritually dead, alienated from God's life (Ephesians 4:18). Jesus Christ, the "second Adam," made possible a level of living that is higher than the first Adam's level before he sinned! We now have the very life of God *in* us! We are not God, as some false teachers teach, but we do partake of His nature! This nature changes our attitudes and makes all believers brothers. There is no distinction between races, former religions (circumcised or uncircumcised), cultures (Barbarians and Scythians were the lowest savages), or social classes (slave or free). The ground is level at the cross. Though we all differ in many ways, we have unity in our diversity. All believers in Jesus have new natures!

Therefore, we must "clothe ourselves" with the attitudes of Jesus:

Compassion — Tender, heartfelt sympathy for others in this technical, mechanical world. This heartless world system has about as much compassion as a computer. We must not treat others like numbers on a screen, but must be compassionate.

Kindness — Benevolence in action, thoughtfulness of others, unselfishness.

Humility — A lowly attitude before God. We have nothing to be boastful about. If we got justice we would be in hell! Instead we have been extended mercy.

Gentleness — A calm attitude toward others.

Patience — Self-restraint in the face of provocation. Bearing insult and injury without retaliation. Accepting wrong without complaint.

Bearing with others — Acceptance of others with their faults. Getting along with those with whom we disagree. Disagree without being disagreeable. Certain things we must believe and others are not as important. Someone has written this prose to help us bear with others:

> In essentials, unity;
> In nonessentials, liberty;
> In all things, charity.

Forgiveness — We must forgive completely because God has forgiven us. We must avoid resentment or retaliation. We must forgive whether others ask for forgiveness or not.

Love — Love holds all other Christian traits together. Love is the basis of all these other graces.

"Let the peace of Christ rule in your hearts," Paul continues. To "rule" means to "umpire," deciding all questions and settling all doubts. The peace of Christ about an issue or an action is a positive factor, while absence of such peace is a negative factor. Man cannot produce the peace of Christ or cultivate it by good works. Only those who trust Christ enjoy His perfect peace. "You will keep in perfect peace him whose mind is steadfast, because he trusts in you" (Isaiah 26:3). We are to be *thankful* in and for *all* things. Only a born-again, Spirit-filled child of God can give thanks to God for all that happens to him in this life with an attitude of gratitude. He does it by letting *the Word of Christ* dwell richly within him. Jesus Christ is the living and enduring Word of God (1 Peter 1:23). The written Word of God reveals Jesus. We must meditate upon the Bible. We must *teach* and *admonish (warn)* fellow Christians. Only by daily saturating our minds with Scripture are we equipped to teach and warn others. As we saturate our minds in God's Word, songs (from Psalms), hymns (other songs), and spiritual songs (praise to God) flow from our hearts. Real joy dominates our hearts! When Christians meet together in large groups, these songs burst forth in praise to God. The Christian church began as a singing church and when joyful praise is lacking, decay has set in. Real worship is enthusiastic, joyful, and pleasing to God.

Whatever we say or do every day is to be done in Jesus' Name with thanksgiving. What does this mean? Paul gives no list of "dos" and "don'ts," but what we do must be under His leadership as directed by the Holy Spirit. Our new nature desires to please Him and the Holy Spirit gives us the power. What a wonderful plan of God!

Read Colossians 3:18-21

The Home
that Pleases God

Wives, submit . . . Husbands, love . . . children, obey . . .
Colossians 3:18-20

THERE IS A CLEAR "division of labor" on a successful football team. Individual differences make certain players better adapted for certain positions. The quarterback must direct the offense and provide leadership. He needs to think clearly, demonstrate leadership, and have good hands and a strong arm. Linemen must block for the ball carrier, so size and strength is an asset for a good lineman. Receivers must get open and catch the ball. Quickness, speed, and good hands are necessities for them. When each player does his job with the abilities he possesses, the team is successful.

Our homes are like a football team. Each "player" — wife, husband, and children — has certain responsibilities and certain abilities. Knowing the importance of a strong home, Paul gives instructions for each "position."

Wives are to submit to the leadership of their husbands. God has established this chain of command. "Submit" is a military term meaning "to line up according to rank." This doesn't mean she is inferior, but she has less authority and different responsibilities from the husband's. Nature and reason, as well as God's clear directives, make these roles evident. In 1 Timothy 2:13, Paul says that the order of creation makes it clear the man is head of the home. However, the wife's submission is "in the Lord." She is not obligated to follow instructions which are contrary to Scripture.

Husbands are to love their wives and not be harsh with them. No bitterness is allowed on the part of the husband. Loving leadership and not dictatorship is encouraged here. Tender, loving care is the best way for a husband to relate to his wife.

Children are to obey their parents. This obedience is to be continual, not just occasional. Children have less experience and less knowledge, so they must trust the judgment of godly parents who care for them. However, this verse is addressed to children. When children mature and leave home, they should honor their parents, but must "cut the apron strings." It seems natural that young adults grow up, move away, support themselves, and make their own decisions.

Ephesians 6:1 tells children to obey parents "in the Lord." Children are to obey when led in ways pleasing to God. When directed to dishonor God (and some godless parents give such orders) a youngster must obey God. Children are to obey "in the Lord," not "in the devil."

Fathers must not embitter, nag or exasperate their children. Kids are prone to frustration and discouragement. By being inconsiderate, too demanding, over-corrective, unjust, or severe, fathers can provoke kids to rebel. Continual fault-finding and never smiling makes children feel they cannot please anyone. It breaks a child's tender spirit and creates numerous problems in his life. Paul's use of "discouragement" means "no passion" or "no ambition." Frustrated kids lose passion and ambition in life. Maybe a reason so many kids are so purposeless today is because of a frustrating home life!

What is your "position" in your home? Whether wife, husband, father, or child, play it God's way. He will bless your efforts to obey Him and your "team" will be a success!

Read Colossians 3:22-4:1

Christian Motivation

Whatever you do, work at it with all your heart, as working for the Lord, not for men . . .

Colossians 3:23

THREE-TIME OLYMPIC gold medalist swimmer Dawn Frasier had to be highly motivated to achieve at world class levels for so long. "I've always believed that the desire must come from within, not as a result of being driven by coaches or parents," she said. Her stellar career is an example of such internal motivation!

The motivation to live for Christ, to please God, and to honor His commands must also come from within. No external list of rules or harsh taskmaster in the form of parent, pastor, or coach is strong enough to empower us to obey God. That power comes only from the Holy Spirit.

Though Scripture does not condone slavery, Paul wrote to Christian slaves in his day, giving them internal motivation to please God. In the ancient world, there were more slaves than free men. In some Roman cities, that ratio was four to one! It was the spread of the gospel that restored human dignity and led to the destruction of slavery. But a slave who became a Christian was not to demand instant freedom. Some had become slaves because of debts owed. Paul did say a slave should get free, if possible. "Were you a slave when you were called? Don't let it trouble you — although if you can gain your freedom, do so" (1 Corinthians 7:21). While they were slaves (workers), Christians were to obey masters (bosses) in everything. The same principle applies today. Those who work for others are to submit to those who sign their paychecks. The Bible says nothing about "collective bargaining" and "strikes" to bully employers into higher wages. Rather, we are told to obey those for whom we work.

We are to submit to our bosses to win their favor. Our job is to help solve our bosses' problems. When we serve our bosses, we increase our chance of better treatment. This service is not to be done for external appearance, but with sincerity of heart and reverence for the Lord.

We must work with all our heart as working for the Lord and not for men. Because King Hezekiah worked with all his heart in obeying and seeking God, he prospered. "In everything that he undertook in the service of God's temple and in obedience to the law and commands, he sought his God and worked wholeheartedly. And so he prospered" (2 Chronicles 31:21). We are not to work because of being forced or constrained, but out of enthusiasm from our very soul (heart). Though sometimes our faithfulness is recognized and temporal rewards are given on earth, God will reward us eternally in heaven. But we will suffer for doing wrong. God has no favorite sons. Human fathers may unwisely favor one son over another, but God loves and consistently disciplines all of His children.

Leaders (bosses) are to be fair with those under them. Every human leader has a boss in Heaven who repays them for their treatment of their followers. Though Christianity and ownership of slaves are incompatible, working off a debt or hiring out for wages are certainly proper. It is the internal motivation of both leader and worker that God sees and rewards. His paycheck for labor and management is out of this world!

Read Colossians 4:2-6

Foundation of a Walk With God

Devote yourselves to prayer, being watchful and thankful.
Colossians 4:2

BOB COUSY WAS A play-making guard on the great Celtic teams of the 1960s. Though he was a great player, he worked hard to establish a solid foundation for his game. "I dribbled by the hour with my left hand when I was young," he said. "I didn't have full control, but I got so I could move the ball back and forth from one hand to the other without breaking the cadence of my dribble. I wasn't dribbling behind my back or setting up any trick stuff, but I was laying the groundwork for it."

A solid foundation is also vital if we are to maintain a consistent walk with God. Paul lists several "building blocks" that are vital to our walk. The first building block is prayer.

Prayer is a practical link to Almighty God. It is our lifeline through which we draw strength from our Creator. Are you devoted to prayer? Do you not only believe intellectually in prayer and the power it makes available, but do you actually pray? It is one thing to talk about prayer or to discuss our needs with each other, but it is something else to actually pray. If all the time spent discussing requests were used to actually *pray,* our lives would be more full!

We are to pray with watchfulness and thankful hearts. What does it mean to watch? It means to stay alert, to be observant of people and events. We are not to have our minds so far in the clouds that we don't know what goes on on earth. We watch so we can pray intelligently.

For what are we to be thankful 1 Thessalonians 5:18 says to be thankful *in* everything and Ephesians 5:20 says be thankful *for* everything. A Sovereign God is guiding our lives from His holy throne. We have much to thank Him for!

Effective prayer is led by the Holy Spirit within us. We are to be constantly in touch with Him as He makes our requests known to the Father. In this way, we pray every moment of the day, simply agreeing with the unspoken "groans" He makes to God the Father (Romans 8:26). A contemporary song says, "We will use the words we know to tell You (God) what an awesome God You are, but words are not enough to tell You of our love so listen to our hearts." That's exactly what it means to pray without ceasing (1 Thessalonians 5:3b)! The Holy Spirit prays through us!

Paul asked others to pray for an open door so he could speak God's truth to people. He wanted prayer that he would make God's Word clear. He wanted to be released from the bondage of prison so he could return to the streets and preach the same gospel that had gotten him put into prison! Until then, he preached to guards and prisoners and some of them believed in Jesus! He had an open door in prison to preach until the prison door opened to let him out!

A true walk with God is a walk in wisdom toward unbelievers (v 5). Believers should live in such a way that unbelievers see Jesus in them and are attracted to Him. We are the world's Bible. Some never read it, but they read *us!* If an unbeliever despises the gospel and refuses to seriously consider Jesus' claims, we must not "cast pearls before swine" (Matthew 7:6). Never should we push the gospel upon those who don't want to know the truth. But we must make the most of every opportunity, for many people *do* want to know God! Solomon said, "He that wins souls is wise" (Proverbs 11:30). Daniel was told, "Those who are wise will shine like the brightness of the heavens, and those who lead many to righteousness, like the stars for ever and ever" (Daniel 12:3). Winning souls is *BIG* business to God!

Finally, believers are to be careful how they speak. At no time should we compromise the gospel, but we must not be terse or speak down to people. Our speech should be kind, humble and full of the grace of God. The tongue has the power of life and death (Proverbs 18:21). It must preserve people as salt preserves meat!

Read Colossians 4:7-18

Character in Adverse Circumstances

. . . that you may know about our circumstances . . .

Colossians 4:8

TENNIS PROFESSIONALS COMPETE with great intensity in a sport where politeness is expected. The designers of Centre Court at Wimbledon wanted to remind all competitors of the importance of character in whatever circumstances they faced. As an athlete enters Centre Court and looks up, he sees these words adapted from a famous work by Kipling: "If you can meet with triumph and disaster and treat those two impostors just the same, if you can do that, you will have class."

Paul had class and great character. He was chained in a Roman prison when he wrote to the Colossians. Yet, with great optimism and with concern for the welfare of others, he warned them against reverting to old ways of believing and acting. He refuted false teaching and exalted the Lord Jesus as sufficient in every trial.

Paul had many friends whom he kept informed of his circumstances. Though he was an outstanding apostle, he never felt superior to other Christians. He needed loyal support as he suffered in prison. Listen to the roll call of friends he lists at the conclusion of his letter:

TYCHICUS — The carrier of the letter, Tychicus was a beloved brother in Christ and a faithful servant.

ONESIMUS — The co-bearer of the letter, Onesimus was a runaway slave who accepted Christ. He also carried Paul's letter to Philemon, from whom he had escaped.

ARISTARCHUS — He was in prison with Paul.

MARK — Once wrongly rejected by Paul, Mark was now commended by him (Acts 15, 2 Timothy 4:11).

Jesus (Justus) — Most Jews had nothing to do with Paul, a fact which hurt him deeply. Justus was one of the few who accepted Christ and helped Paul.

Epaphras — A Colossian who visited Paul and stayed with him. He loved the believers in Colosse and prayed fervently for them, knowing the subtlety of the false teachers there.

Luke — A medical doctor who loved Paul and often traveled with him. Luke was probably a Gentile.

Demas — Demas later deserted Paul for this present world (2 Timothy 4:10-11).

Nympha and the brothers at Laodicea — Nympha hosted church meetings in a private house. For the first 300 years of Christianity, there were no church buildings!

Paul's letter was intended to be circulated to other church assemblies after being read by the Colossians. It is still in circulation as part of Scripture today! As he signed his name at the end of the letter, the chain on his wrist probably clanked. It reminded him of his suffering on behalf of Christ and he wrote, "Remember my chains . . ." (4:18). He wanted the Colossians to remember the price he was paying for preaching the truth that salvation is free to all who trust Christ. As he had opened his letter with grace, he closes with grace. What character Paul manifested in the adversities of life!

1 TIMOTHY
Introduction

NEAR THE BEGINNING OF 64 AD, Paul was released from a
Roman prison as he was "off the D.L!" However, he would
soon be rearrested and beheaded. Resuming his mission of
sharing Christ with the world, Paul headed for Macedonia.
But he didn't neglect to write personal letters to Timothy, his
close friend at Ephesus and to Titus, a Gentile convert who
had learned from Paul and spoken for him in Corinth (Galatians 2:3, 2 Corinthians 2:7-8). Paul's brief messages on
leadership to these men are relevant to leaders today.

Timothy had a Greek father and a Jewish mother named
Eunice (Acts 16:2, 2 Timothy 1:5). He had been taught Scripture since his youth (2 Timothy 3:15). Paul had visited
Timothy's childhood home in Lystra, boldly preached the
gospel, been stoned, and left for dead! These events had a
profound impact upon Timothy and may have led to his
conversion to Christ!

False teachers (Gnostics) had invaded the Ephesian
church, which now met in the school of Tyrannus (probably in
the gym!). Timothy was standing for truth against these
heretics . Paul advised him how to handle the situation
(1 Timothy 3:14-15). The *creed* of the church and her *conduct*
before the world are themes in his letters.

Good leadership is vital to an organization. Without it,
there is no structure or direction. Leaders must be men of
faith. They must be motivated by love. Churches have different organizational forms, but without faith and love they
become only "religious clubs." With faith and love, the form of
government becomes less significant. The leader of a church
is under the authority of the Lord Jesus Christ, and his role is
to discover the will of the Lord, not to dictate his own will.

Timothy may have been naturally timid and easily intimidated. He was relatively young. Paul constantly "spurned him
to action" as a defender of the faith. Paul's "leadership letters"
have encouraged millions since 64 AD. May his principles of
leadership continue to guide our creed and our conduct as we
lead others to follow Jesus.

Read 1 Timothy 1:1-11

Christian Leadership

Paul, an apostle of Christ Jesus by the command of God our Savior and of Christ Jesus our hope.

1 Timothy 1:1

MOTHER TERESA WAS A LEADER with a purpose. She was so committed to the purpose of helping India's poor that when she won the Nobel Prize, she refused to go accept more recognition because it interfered with her work. She was not in the business of accepting prizes, but of serving Calcutta's poor. Christian leadership traits "oozed out" of Mother Teresa.

Leadership traits are "oozing out" of Paul's first letter to Timothy. Paul begins by asserting his calling to be an apostle by the command of Jesus Christ. He had a sense of purpose and destiny. Paul didn't just decide one day, "I think I'll be an apostle." He knew God had commanded him to give out the gospel. As a "sent one," Paul saw purpose in everything that happened to him. He had authority because he was *under* authority!

A leader stays with a task. Timothy may have wanted to quit when the going got tough, but Paul told him to "stay put" (v 3). Persistence is a real mark of leadership.

A leader boldly rebukes wrongdoing. What a lesson for us in the climate of moral relativism today! Wrong is still wrong, and a leader doesn't remain silent with evil in progress.

A leader must not be side-tracked by the fraud and irrelevance of Gnostics, who debated myths and endless genealogies. They said a good creator had created a bad creator and a long line of angelic beings in between. It was their version of Star Wars' "dark side" vs. "light side" of the force! Other false systems (Judaism) mixed law and grace, perverting both. These false teachers didn't know what they were talking about (v 7). The purpose of the law was to show sinners their sin. Guy King says the law reveals three things: "We ought. We haven't. We can't!" Therefore, we cry out to be saved by *grace!* Christian leaders must not be side-tracked or confused. They must know the truth and teach it.

94

A good leader is respected by those he leads (Acts 16:2-5). He seeks a higher good (Philippians 2:19-23). False teachers, on the other hand, had ambitious pride, exalted ego, worthless curiosity and incompetent, aimless preaching.

A good leader loves those he leads. This love comes from a pure heart, a good conscience and sincere faith. A pure heart results from confession of sin and a focus upon Jesus. The conscience can be set like a thermostat so it isn't reliable, but we must not go against its warnings. Sincere faith must be placed in the right object. Jesus is that "object," for correct belief is the basis for correct behavior.

Some people had wandered away ("exkrepo," a medical term for "twisted out of joint" like an arm out of socket) from the truth. They caused pain to the entire body. They went from the one extreme of asceticism (a stoic denial of all desire) to the other of license (total fulfillment of all desires). Like any good leader, Timothy was to show them back to the truth. Jesus Christ, the greatest leader of all, is that Truth!

Read 1 Timothy 1:12-20

From Worst to First by God's Grace

Here is a trustworthy saying that deserves full acceptance: Christ Jesus came into the world to save sinners — of whom I am the worst.

1 Timothy 1:15

IN 1991, THE MINNESOTA TWINS won the American League pennant after finishing the previous year in last place. The Atlanta Braves also went from "worst to first" that year. When the two teams met in the World Series, Minnesota went on to beat the Braves, four games to three.

Paul was the premier apostle in the New Testament, but he went from "worst to first" only by the grace of God! Paul had brought terror into the lives of early Christians. It is likely he was one of the Pharisees who taunted Jesus as He died on the cross. His contempt broke out in terrible violence against Jesus' followers and he persecuted ("hunted down like animals") them. No Pharisee knowingly slandered God, but Paul blasphemed Jesus, not knowing He was God in human flesh!

Then Paul received God's grace ("undeserved favor") and he was called to serve Jesus! Unlike the German philosopher Nietzche who said, "If you could prove God to me, I would believe him all the less." Paul had acted in ignorance. Paul didn't' just "turn over a new leaf." He was radically changed and he was so thankful! He becomes an example of the unlimited patience of Jesus Christ and Paul gave the Lord Jesus great honor and glory (v 17).

Anyone who is really saved from sin must be humble and exceedingly thankful. Someone has said, "The beginning of greatness is to be little; it increases as we become less and it is perfect when we become nothing." Paul admitted he was nothing. The persecutor who had denied Jesus, now embraced him as the only God!

Nevertheless, Paul boldly instructed Timothy on leadership. Timothy "fights the good fight of faith and good conscience." The enemy of our souls has declared war and we fight by faith. Only by confessing all known sin can we maintain a clear conscience. God had called Timothy via an earlier prophecy (v 18) and he dare not forget it! He must continue to rebuke the false teachers in Ephesus.

Evidently, two men had rejected faith and sinned against their consciences. They had "shipwrecked" their faith and Paul called for their discipline, probably by excommunication from fellowship with the believers. This was severe discipline in the early church. Satan's realm is dangerous and there was no completed New Testament Scriptures, radio preachers, or Bible studies to attend. The sea of this world is littered with "shipwrecked" ministers today. But true leaders continue to stand by faith without violating their consciences.

Paul, the worst of sinners, didn't talk about what he did for God. He preached about what God had done for him! The Lord Jesus didn't come to save good people. There are none! He didn't come to be the world's greatest teacher (though He was). He didn't come to set a good moral example (which He did). He came to save sinners from their sin! If He could save Paul, He can save anyone!

Read 1 Timothy 2:1-8

A Rift Healed

For there is one God and one mediator between God and men,
the man Christ Jesus, who gave himself as a ransom for all
men — the testimony given in its proper time.

1 Timothy 2:5-6

ADRIAN CONSTANTINE "CAP" ANSON was the Babe Ruth of
his time. He played and managed in the late 1800s and was
baseball's first 3000-hit player. But his opposition to black
players was a source of comment through every league in the
country. Before Anson, some black players had played major
league baseball. But while managing the Chicago White
Stockings in a game against Toledo, Anson saw Fleetwood
Walker on the diamond and yelled, "Get that nigger off the
field." According to historian Art Rust, Jr., Anson's popularity
and power in baseball almost single-handedly kept the black
man from white baseball until Branch Rickey brought black
and white together in 1947. The great rift in professional
baseball has since been healed.

Our sin has caused a great rift between God and man.
Branch Rickey couldn't heal this rift, but Jesus Christ the
Creator, became man to bring the Father and His creation
together! He accomplished this by His shed blood on the
cross! He constantly prays for us according to God's will
(Hebrews 7:25). He is our advocate, speaking to the Father in
our defense when the enemy accuses us (1 John 2:1-3). What
an advocate! What a defender!

There is only one way to God and He is the Way (Acts
4:12). Joseph Smith is not the way, nor is Mary, another
saint, an angel or a clergyman. We are not the way, for we
cannot rescue ourselves! He *gave* Himself for us. He was not
tricked by the devil, nor overpowered by the Romans. He was
not a victim of circumstances. He willingly laid down His life
so we could know God! And He still prays for us in our daily
struggles with sin, self, and Satan. What a Savior!

God has established human government to keep relative
peace in a sin-filled world. Government prevents us from

97

destroying ourselves by civil war, anarchy, and rioting. It is easier to preach truth in peacetime than in chaos. We are to pray for our leaders, no matter who they are. We must not be cut off from the politics of governing, for human leaders make decisions that affect us. Notice, we must pray *for* leaders, not *to* them. Rome worshiped the emperor. When Paul wrote to Timothy, it was six years before the Romans destroyed Jerusalem. In July, 64 AD, Rome burned and Nero's intense persecution of Christians began. Yet, Paul said we are to earnestly plead for all in authority. However bad their leader-ship may be, it is better than anarchy.

God wants all men to be saved (v 4). This is one part of His will that won't happen. Tony Evans explains it this way: God has purchased a Coke (salvation) for everyone ever born and offered it to everyone. Everyone refused His offer! So, He personally selected and called some to accept the Coke. All He selected and called came and received the Coke. He wanted all to be saved but since not all would come, He chose some. Whoever chooses Jesus has been chosen by God!

God tells men to pray with holy hands lifted up. Body language is important. It reveals our inner attitude. We must get our minds off self and on to God. Our lives must be holy, free from unconfessed sin. We must have healthy human relationships, free from outbursts of anger. Broken relation-ships affect one's ability to pray and to lead others in prayer.

God has called us to be saved. He has provided a media-tor, the Lord Jesus Christ. He tells us to pray for our leaders and instructs us how to do it. Under His authority, we have authority to lead others.

Read 1 Timothy 2:9-15

Leadership and Ladies

But women will be saved through childbearing — if they continue in faith, love, and holiness with propriety.

1 Timothy 2:15

PAM POSTEMA WAS A MINOR LEAGUE UMPIRE attempting to get to the major leagues. Bob Knepper was a pitcher for the Houston Astros. Bob got little support from his Astro teammates when he voiced his belief that women should not umpire. He found nothing wrong with her work, but said, "There are some things that men shouldn't do and some things that a woman shouldn't do. I think umpiring is one of them. I have a belief that God has intended men and women to be different. It's a physical thing. I don't think women were created by God to be a physical, hard person. I think God created women to be feminine."

God is big on roles. He has created all of us equal in value (Galatians 3:28), but He has certain roles for each. He gave specific assignments to ladies for their ultimate fulfillment and joy.

First, a lady's *deeds* should outshine her *dress.* It is good to be well-dressed and attractive, but a lady should be more known for her character than her appearance. Appearances can be deceiving and shallow. Temple prostitutes in ancient religions exhibited themselves to attract men. But pagan culture must not establish Christian fashion! A woman should not be gaudy, dressed like she's coming to a carnival or a fashion show when she comes to worship God. When we pray or worship, the focus is upon God, not self.

Second, a lady must submit (1 Corinthians 14:34-35) to male authority. God has assigned to men positions of authority and leadership in His church. Ladies are to learn in "hesychia" (not silence, but a settled down and undisturbed manner). There are two reasons why ladies are not to teach men: Adam was created as head of the family and Eve sinned through the deception of Satan. She fell by taking unwarranted leadership, making a decision to disobey God without consulting her husband. Even today, false teachers love to talk to women alone, without the caution of their husbands.

Third, a lady must lead children (1 Timothy 3:15). She is saved from having no position, power, or purpose by teaching kids to be godly — provided she continues to live a holy life. In teaching children and in teaching younger women (Titus 2:4), a lady wields great power and authority. It has been said, "The hand that rocks the cradle rules the world." No one can influence a person like a godly mother, and a lady finds deepest satisfaction as a wife and mother. The fastest, most effective way to turn society to God is for ladies to fulfill their God-given leadership roles.

A lady must not attempt to do what God has assigned a man to do. And a man *cannot* do what a lady was created to do. May we have more "lady leadership" in lives of children and young women.

Read 1 Timothy 3:1-16

Leadership Qualifications

Here is a trustworthy saying, "If anyone sets his heart on being an overseer, he desires a noble task."

1 Timothy 3:1

IN 1999, KEN GRIFFEY refused to take a leadership role with the Seattle Mariners, even though he was a great player. "Everyone decides for himself when it is their time to lead," Griffey said. "You can do what you want, as long as it doesn't affect me. 'Leader' is just a title, and I don't have a problem with anything as long as we win. It's a case of don't interfere with my space and I won't interfere with yours. I'm not a leader, but I'm not a follower."

Too many men like Ken Griffey, Jr. refuse to lead today. God says it is commendable to desire leadership roles in His church and it seems many qualifications for leadership are relevant in government and business. He develops leaders, but we must identify them. He sets up leaders, not to "rule" but to *care for* those who come to Christ. No one man is to be a dictator. A plurality of leaders (called bishops, overseers, or elders) are to lead and manage, while others (deacons or deaconesses - Romans 16:1) are called to serve. The qualifications to lead are listed in four areas: character, home life, teaching ability and experience.

The first quality necessary in a leader is moral character. Leaders must be above reproach. They may be accused by slander, but must not be guilty or they disqualify themselves from leadership. Leaders must be temperate, be self-controlled, respectable, not controlled by alcohol, gentle when provoked, and not ready to quarrel over every little thing. They must not be greedy or dishonest, for they will handle public funds. Their reputations must be good, for Satan will expose every flaw to the world! They must be men of respect and not frivolous (Ecclesiastes 10:1), sincere and not given to either flattery or slander. They must be hospitable to everyone. A good leader cannot be a hermit.

Second, a leader must have a healthy home life. He must be monogamous, contrary to the polygamy of false religions (Mormonism) which leads to heartache, tragedy and chaos. Clearly, if a polygamist got saved (as sometimes happens in pagan cultures), he could not become a church leader. Paul seems to encourage marriage in these verses. He probably had been married, for he could not have been a member of the Sanhedrin without marriage. A leader's wife must be worthy of respect. Wives must not be "malicious talkers," but temperate and trustworthy. A slanderous wife can ruin her husband's effectiveness and disqualify him from leadership! He must manage his family well, having respectful children. He leads without undue hardness or laxity.

Third, a leader must be able to teach. Both his mind and his heart must be set upon God's Word. He knows where to find the answers to the problems of life in Scripture. He grasps the deep truths of the faith with a clear conscience.

Finally, a leader must be experienced and tested (v 10). He must not be a "rookie," having just come to faith in Christ. It takes time to shed both the world's standards and religious legalism, whichever has been in his past. Rapid promotion may cause him to become proud and it was pride that caused the devil's downfall! Lucifer sought a high position for which he was unqualified and he became Satan — "the Adversary!"

Paul quoted an early hymn about the mystery of Christianity (v 16). The mystery that Jesus came, lived a perfect life, and returned to heaven is great. These truths cannot be discovered by reason because they are above reason. They cannot be discovered in nature, though nature reveals there is a Creator. The mystery is revealed by God to His church. Good character, a strong family, solid teaching and experience enable leaders to protect these truths.

Read 1 Timothy 4:1-16

Serious Training

. . . . train yourself to be godly . . .

1 Timothy 4:7

PARRY O'BRIEN WAS a great shot-putter. His father used to say he had "more determination than four mules." After one meet in Fresno, California, Parry stayed on the track and practiced for two hours, barely making his flight home to Santa Monica at 1:30 AM. At 3:00 AM, Parry's father was awakened by the sound of heavy thuds outside. Parry was practicing under a street light. "I think I've discovered something," he said to his dad. And he practiced until four o'clock in the morning.

Parry changed his style of delivery and became the first to put the shot 60 feet. He always found time or made time to practice. "I don't quit until my hands are bleeding," he once said.

Though he was now in his mid-thirties, Timothy needed the serious training advocated by "coach" Paul if he was to be fulfill his potential. Paul encouraged him to "gymnaze" himself to be godly. Timothy understood the reference to physical fitness, for the Ephesians loved sports. Ephesus had a 100,000 seat stadium which sometimes hosted the Olympics.

Though the benefits of fitness are valuable in this life, godliness is valuable now and forever! Godliness is the object of Timothy's training (and ours, too!). Godliness doesn't just happen by sitting in church, any more than sitting in the weight room looking at weights makes one physically strong!

We cannot drift into godliness because the tide is *against* us. It comes at the cost of great effort!

Paul's "training tips" were important because after he wrote ("later times") there would be a great falling away from the faith. This "apostasy" had already begun and Gnosticism (austere withdrawal from the world *or* self-indulgence in the world) flooded the church in the second century. The Spirit of God spoke clearly to indicate that deceiving spirits would lead many astray. Demons would actually teach through lying, hypocritical human teachers. These people masqueraded as apostles, claiming to know God (2 Corinthians 11:13-15). Their sensation of right and wrong was deadened, as if seared with a branding iron. They had suppressed their consciences so long that they didn't speak anymore. This became Satan's standard operating procedure and he still uses it to deceive people in cults (Ephesians 6:12). Their mistakes are not innocent. They deliberately deceive. Legalistic rules prohibiting marriage of priests and eating of certain foods result. Spiritists teach that eating meat hinders contact with the spirits and Hindus avoid meat because of belief in reincarnation.

Timothy trained hard to combat these enemies of truth. Likewise, we must pray, study Scripture, stay near godly examples, and talk to others about Jesus. We don't grow by doing nothing! We must "strive" ("agonize as an athlete") for godliness because our hope is set upon God (v 10). Our hope is not in philosophy, false gods, self, or in other men. Our hope will be fulfilled because it is placed in the living Go! It is He who preserves all men and saves all who believe. (Note: All men *can* be saved, but only those who believe *are* saved).

Christianity is *discipline* as well as *doctrine* and Timothy may have been a little timid (1 Corinthians 16:10). Paul encouraged him not to be intimidated by older believers, but to read Scripture, to preach and to teach boldly. Just as the leaders in Ezra's day "made it clear and gave meaning so that people could understand" (Nehemiah 8:8), Timothy was to expound God's Word. He must not neglect his God-given gift. Like a team breaking the huddle, elders had partnered with him with hands together as they prayed for him (v 14). Now, Timothy must "give himself wholly" to his work, with enthusiasm that comes from God. If he persevered in training, he could save himself and others from the false teachings taught by demons. Go get 'em, Timothy!

Leading a Variety of People

. . . do nothing out of favoritism.

1 Timothy 5:21

A GOOD LEADER REMAINS open to the opinions of everyone he would lead. Followers must feel free to voice their concerns to a leader. As John Madden, former Oakland Raiders' coach has said, "You have to hear things you really don't want to hear; you must look at things you really don't want to see."

People in any group differ from each other. We all have different backgrounds, abilities, and interests. We are of equal value before God, but we certainly are not created equal! Paul advised Timothy precisely how to lead the variety of people who followed Christ.

Older men are to be led tactfully. Younger leaders must not appear to be brash "know-it-alls," but must entreat seniors privately with humility. It never works to be a dictator.

Younger men are to be led with consideration as younger brothers. We like to protect and encourage younger brothers.

Older women must be respected. Motherhood deserves the utmost respect, for none of us would be here without our mothers!

Widows over 60 years of age are to be supported by their church if they have no family to do so and if they have lived and continue to live godly lives. This is God's welfare program.

Young widows are advised to remarry and have children. Their calling is to make a home. No man can do the job of home-making like a woman.

Elder men who teach are to be paid generously. Oxen who treaded on wheat to separate it from straw in the ancient harvest were allowed to eat some of the crop. Similarly, elder teachers must be paid (Deuteronomy 25:4).

God knows that human leaders are criticized. But only if two or three witnesses are willing to step forward and prove their accusation should criticism be listened to. If a leader's sin has been public, it should be rebuked publicly so others won't repeat it. Private sins are to be confronted, confessed, and rebuked privately. Everyone must be disciplined without favoritism.

Leadership must not be given to a "rookie" in the faith. Laying on of hands indicates a partnership, like giving a "high five." Make sure a man has some experience and knows what to teach before making him a leader!

Timothy must have abstained from alcohol. But noticing that those who drank a little alcohol had fewer illnesses, Paul recommended a little wine as medicine. No one knew about germs in Paul's day. Today, our medicines do wonderful jobs in preventing sickness and abstinence is the best policy.

Paul reminded Timothy that no one gets away with sin. All our deeds — good or bad — will be ultimately revealed. Either we judge ourselves or God will do it (1 Corinthians 11:31)! We must repent and make restitution for sin. God will reward good deeds.

Slaves are instructed to serve with respect. A very high percentage of people were slaves in Paul's day. To revolt would cause great bloodshed and make it difficult to spread the gospel. The solution to slavery (and all social evils) is the conversion of individuals to Christ and to His way of thinking. Wherever real Christianity has gone, the vile practice of slavery has eventually been abolished. Repentance ("to change one's mind") results in freedom. All are of equal value before God and it is probable that some slaves were leaders over masters in early Christian meetings.

What a diverse group Timothy had to lead. But we have the same diversity in churches today. Only the Spirit of God can bring harmony. But when God's playbook is obeyed in the power of the Spirit, victory is inevitable!

Read 1 Timothy 6:3-10

The Emptiness of Greed

For the love of money is a root of all kinds of evil.

1 Timothy 6:10

ACQUIRING THINGS has never satisfied the human soul. The more we feed on greed, the more the hunger grows. John D. Rockfeller said, "I have made many millions, but they have brought me no happiness." John Jacob Astor left five million, but at the end of his life lamented, "I am the most miserable man on earth." Henry Ford longed for the happier days of doing a mechanic's job. Andrew Carnegie commented, probably from personal experience, "Millionaires seldom smile." Deion Sanders hadn't even driven his new $275 thousand Lamborghini one mile before he realized, "No, that's not it. That's not what I'm looking for. It's got to be something else. I'm so hungry!"

Most Americans fight a perpetual war in their hearts. The love of money, which produces desire for more "stuff," wages war against godly contentment with the things we already own! Paul warns Timothy and the Ephesian church to beware of succumbing to continual greed for more possessions.

False teaching is at the heart of many money problems. And even correct teaching with the motive of "fleecing the flock" of undiscerning Christians occurs today in America. Huge financial "ministries" take millions from naive believers and squander it in luxury while the world starves. It is not wrong for a preacher to accept money, but money must not be his motive. False teachers are those who don't agree to sound instruction. They aren't even close to it, due not to innocent mistakes but to intentional deception. False teachers have inflated egos (conceit), understand nothing (without realizing it), and quarrel continually. Their hidden envy of others produces strife (open envy), malicious talk (slander), evil suspicion (twisting and judging others' motives), and constant friction with others like them.

Godliness (real Christianity) with contentment is great gain, far surpassing financial gain. Cicero, a Roman philoso-

106

pher, said "contentment is great gain." But men must not be content in sin, for their destiny is hell without the Lord Jesus Christ. We need Jesus and godliness!

Job said, "Naked came I from my mother's womb, and naked I will depart" (Job 1:21). All our financial gain will be lost. Clement of Rome realized earth's journey is temporary and said, "We must be content with the travel allowance given us by Christ." Howard Hughes discovered this truth, but too late! Alexander the Great, who held the scepter of world power along with great riches, said, "When I am dead, carry me forth on my bier, with my hands not wrapped in cloth, but laid outside, so that all may see that they are empty."

We must be content with daily food and covering (a roof over us and clothes on us). Intense desire for wealth destroys contentment. The rich must not trust in their riches, but do good with them (vs 17-18). Too many "set their hearts upon riches (Psalm 62:10). They have fallen into temptation, become trapped by their desires, and been ruined (James 1:14). Matthew Henry says, "When the devil sees which way their lusts carry them, he will soon bait his hook accordingly." We must pray "lead us not into temptation" and keep focused upon Jesus.

Love of money (not money itself) is a root of evils like theft, intemperance, selfishness, and the ignoring of God. Even poor people can love money. Love of money destroys faith in God and causes the soul to shrivel up. People who love money will do almost anything to get more. Worries of life and deceit of riches choke out God's Word from our lives (Matthew 13:22). Neglect of God starves the soul and sets men up for grief. Thinking they have more important things to do, people who love money avoid Christians, rarely pray, and never study God's Word. Clergymen are affected as well as laymen. Doctors, lawyers, street people, and pro athletes can all be affected. They "pierce themselves" with many griefs as certainly as if they wore a spiked collar or a crown of thorns! As Ryle says, "There is trouble in getting money, anxiety in keeping it, temptations in using it, guilt in abusing it, sorrow in losing it, and perplexity in disposing of it!"

Godliness with contentment must win its daily war with love of money. Which is winning with you?

Read 1 Timothy 6:11-21

Instructions to a Leader

Fight the good fight of the faith. Take hold of the eternal life to which you were called when you made your good confession in the presence of many witnesses.

1 Timothy 6:12

BENJAMIN HOOKS SAID, "He who thinketh he leadeth and hath no one following him is only taking a walk!" Good leaders have had to learn to lead, and before a man becomes a leader, he must be a good follower. Even after becoming a leader, he must remain under authority. There will always be other human leaders and a sovereign God above every one.

Paul concluded his first "leadership letter" to Timothy with instructions to flee some things, pursue others, fight the good fight, command some people, guard the gospel, and to turn away from godless chatter. He addressed Timothy as a "man of God" (one who makes men think of and glorify God) as opposed to a "man of sin" (one who makes men think of sin).

A good leader must *run* from sins like conceit (v 4), impurity (v 5), discontentment (vs 6-8), foolish and harmful lusts (v 9), and love of money (v 10). He flees these things not as a coward, but in obedience to the Master Coach, just as Joseph fled when propositioned by Potiphar's wife.

A good leader *pursues* righteousness (integrity with other people), godliness (integrity with God), faith (in God and His Word), love for others, endurance and gentleness.

A good leader must *fight* the good fight of the faith. Like an athlete, he contends against false teaching without being a contentious person. He lives out the eternal life he has been given. As Ronald Ward says, "He strains every nerve at any cost in order to win." He out thinks and outlives the enemies of the gospel to reach others first with God's truth.

A good leader *takes hold* of eternal life. He has life in Christ, but must grasp it practically. Plato told of a man who owned an aviary. One day he went in and grabbed one of his birds, taking firm hold of it. That is how Timothy was to grasp the eternal life he possessed. He had made a good confession

108

when he publicly confessed Christ, "burning his bridges" of retreat. Now, he must press on! In the sight of God (not Caesar), who gives life to everything, Jesus made the good confession before Pilate, proclaiming Himself King over a kingdom not of this world. Caesar was "politically correct and popular, but Jesus is coming to rule His world! The blessed and only Ruler sovereignly controls all things! Though today He is the Rejected One, He will soon become the Ruling One. He is King of kings and Lord of lords! He alone has immortality to confer. He lives in unapproachable light, for no one can approach Him without being vaporized! No one has seen God's essence and lived to tell about it! Jesus alone has revealed His nature by taking on a body!

Timothy was to *command* rich Christians in Ephesus (Acts 20:33-35) not to become arrogant or to hope in wealth. Most of us in North America are wealthy, when compared to the rest of the world. But wealth is uncertain. It can be lost through theft, deterioration, or disaster. Money can provide a splendid funeral but it cannot prepare us to meet God! It is given us to generously share with others. It is not wrong to be rich and we can *send* our wealth on to heaven by giving to others. There it will await us as a reward. We only keep what we give away! Let us exchange the temporary for the eternal.

A good leader must *guard* the gospel of the grace of God like money is guarded by a bank. False teachers would pervert the message with "godless chatter" and false "knowledge" (esoteric ideas or so-called "science" which denies the Creator). Timothy must *turn away* from such fruitless conjecture and dwell upon God's truth.

Paul has described faithful leadership. Christian leaders are to follow his instructions for they come from God Himself. His principles protect the gospel and take many to victory in the game of life!

2 TIMOTHY
Introduction

PAUL IS BACK ON THE "D.L." He has been arrested by Nero during the Great Persecution of Christians of 64-68 AD. It is 66 or 67 AD, and Paul awaits beheading in a cold, dark Roman prison. Only Luke is with him. His last note is a second "leadership letter" to Timothy, to encourage him during hardship.

Loyalty is a characteristic of leadership. Paul emphasized loyalty in this letter. He encouraged Timothy to be loyal in suffering (Chapter 1), loyal in service to God (Chapter 2), loyal when others fall away from the faith (Chapter 3), and loyal to Paul though others had deserted him (Chapter 4).

Paul warns Timothy against a complete "apostasy," an apostasy which had already begun. What is apostasy? Webster says it is a "total desertion of the principles of faith." It is deliberate error. An apostate person knows truth and repudiates it. Because of this apostasy, Paul emphasizes the Word of God more in this letter than in any other.

Today, apostasy has exploded throughout organized Christianity. The great departure from the faith is not yet total among organized religion, but it will be as soon as the true believers depart to be with Jesus! Jesus predicted the apostasy (Luke 18:8) as sure as Paul wrote of the departure (rapture) of believers (1 Thessalonians 4:16-17).

Social programs will not transform the world. The moral nature of man is absolutely corrupt and cannot be fixed. It must be exchanged for a new nature which does not sin. That is the message of real Christianity. Faith in Christ is the only thing that transforms human lives. We are not on our way upward apart from Christ. Natural man is a doomed sinner. But Almighty God creates out of nothing. When man realizes he is nothing, God will remake him! That's the message of the gospel Paul preached and the message he tells Timothy to protect with loyalty and enthusiasm.

Read 2 Timothy 1:1-7

Power for Leadership

For God did not give us a spirit of timidity, but a spirit of power, of love, and of self-discipline.

2 Timothy 1:7

NOT ONLY WAS WALT WEISS signed by the Atlanta Braves during the winter of 1998 to help on the field, but also to help chemistry in the clubhouse. A born-again Christian, Weiss is steady and mild-mannered, yet competitive. "I think it's important to have a handful of guys that have been around and are basically good leaders," he said. "Some guys call clubhouse meetings to clear the air, and that may be good once in a while, but I think it's kind of overrated. Veterans playing the game hard, being professional, and showing a good example has a lot more impact."

Paul was a great apostle and veteran leader. But he was not an apostle by his own choosing. It was God's sovereign will that he share the gospel and he served with a pure conscience. This means not that he never sinned, but that the underlying direction and motivation of his life was to obey and please God. Therefore, he habitually recognized and confessed sin (1 John 1:9). He was a model of leadership.

' Timothy loved and honored Paul. He apparently broke down into tears when the old apostle was hastily arrested and returned to a Roman prison. Though a prisoner awaiting execution, Paul never ceased to pray for Timothy. He had little else to do! Much of Timothy's power was certainly due to the prayers of Paul while he was a chained prisoner!

Timothy may have been timid and discouraged over Paul's imprisonment over false leaders, or by the falling away of Christians. Paul suggested a remedy. First, he was to "fan into flame" the gifts of God. Many Christians allow the wonderful gift of the Holy Spirit to lie dormant within them. They grieve or quench Him and their fire dies down to smoldering embers. They never develop their spiritual gifts (teaching, giving, exhorting others). The Spirit of God is "stirred up" within us by praise, worship, and obedience. His gifts do not function automatically. They depend upon our current relationship with Jesus. We "fan them into flame" by discovering and using them.

God's Spirit is not one of timidity (cowardice). We become fearful when we take our eyes off the Lord. Some people fear the future, possible failure, man's opinion of them, suffering, or rejection. Some even fear success! During World War II, Churchill said Britains had only fear itself to fear. Godly people do not fear what may happen (v 7), for we have a powerful God. He cannot use servants who cower before the worldly crowd. Timothy was in Ephesus, the "Sin City" of the world. But God's Spirit could give him power to serve boldly, to endure, to suffer and to die if necessary. God's power gives aggressive energy in the face of difficulty.

God's Spirit also gives love for God and for others. He causes us to serve enthusiastically. He causes us to forget self and focus on other people. His Spirit of love makes us bold.

Finally, God's Spirit gives us self-discipline. He helps us not to react hastily or foolishly. He helps us to decide with balanced judgment. He frees us from slavery to our emotions, to our appetites, or to our bodies. We must live self-controlled lives. Many need this advice today.

The fire has died down in many American believers. We don't follow Christ as closely as we should, we don't pray feverishly, and we don't faithfully study His Word for direction. We must boldly "stir up the flame," even if we are in the minority.

Read 2 Timothy 1:8-18

The Suffering of a Leader

Yet I am not ashamed, because I know whom I have believed, and am convinced that he is able to guard what I have entrusted to him for that day.

2 Timothy 1:12

BEING A LEADER has never been easy. This is especially true in America, where we idolize the leaders and root for the underdogs to knock him off! Coaches are only as good as their most recent game, for fickle fans (and administrators) have a way of turning on them!

It has also never been easy to be a Christian. The Lord Jesus warned that we would suffer in this world (John 15:18, 16:33). In 64 AD, the Emperor Nero (a madman) burned Rome and blamed the Christians. Preaching the gospel became against the law. Because of preaching Christ, Paul was thrown into prison. His friends in Asia (modern Turkey) refused to travel to Rome to testify on his behalf. The personal danger for Christians was great, as thousands were brutally martyred.

Paul called himself a "prisoner of our Lord" because it was for Christ he suffered. The emperor claimed to be "Lord." But Christ alone was Paul's Lord. He served a living Christ Jesus who allowed him to be incarcerated in a cold Roman prison for an eternal purpose. Yet, Paul had great confidence in the God who cared for him. He said, "I *know* (Gr. Oida) with absolute knowledge the One I have believed." He was convinced God was able to guard (a military term) what he had *entrusted* (a banking term meaning "to deposit") to Him until "that day" of ultimate accounting (when Jesus returns to reward us). Paul may not live long, but he knew God would take care of him and reward his work.

A man named Onesiphorus ("help-bringer") had searched diligently until he found Paul in prison. Onesiphorus may have been an Ephesian businessman who was loyal to Paul when it was unpopular and dangerous. Both men were unashamed of suffering and Paul asked Timothy to adopt the same attitude. Their suffering was according to God's plan. Matthew Henry says if we merited salvation, it would be hard to suffer because of it. But since salvation is by the free grace of God, we must not think it too much to suffer because of it! God devised His plan of salvation before time began. His plan is to save all who believe in His Son, the Lord Jesus Christ. His purpose is to abolish spiritual death (separation from God). Physical death has become the gate through which believers pass from this sinful, trouble-filled world into perfect peace and purity. It is impossible to earn salvation by the things we do. This is the message of the gospel.

Paul was a "herald" of this gospel. A "herald" is one who makes an announcement as ordered by another. Paul asked Timothy to guard the gospel from distortion, dilution, deletion, or addition. It would have been easy to compromise the gospel to escape suffering. All Timothy had to do was tell people they could be saved by doing good works. Then their flesh would be satisfied and they would feel like they deserved salvation. Like everyone else, they could take a pinch of incense and throw it on the altar to Caesar proclaiming "Caesar is Lord." Persecution would stop. But that is a lie. Man is a lost sinner bound for eternity in Hell apart from the Lord Jesus Christ. That is the gospel Paul preached and it was a pattern for sound teaching.

There is something wrong when a Christian becomes too popular with this dying world. Samuel Rutherford said, "If you were not strangers here, the hounds of the world would not bark at you." The world regards faith in a crucified Jesus as folly. It makes no sense to the unregenerate mind. But to those who are being saved, He is the only Mediator between God and man. God is satisfied with Him. Are you?

Read 2 Timothy 2:1-7

Endurance of a Leader

Endure hardship with us like a good soldier of Christ Jesus.
2 Timothy 2:3

JOE HARRIS IS the only pitcher to pitch 24 innings in a game and lose. On September 1, 1906, Harris threw 24 innings for the Red Sox before losing 4-1 to the Philadelphia A's. In 1906, Joe was 2-21. In eight of those games his team was shut out. In his three-year career, Harris was 3-30. Heartache and loss became commonplace for him.

We all suffer heartache and loss in a wicked world, so endurance becomes vital for leaders. The apostle Paul gave Timothy much advice in how to live and he "practiced what he preached."

First, Paul said to "be strong in the grace that is in Christ Jesus." Paul liked to discuss *strength* and he loved to discuss *grace*. He tells us to let ourselves be made strong (passively) by the grace of God as we cooperate with God. We cannot grit our teeth and live a Christian life on our own, as if we were performing a power lift in the weight room. Just as we were saved by the grace of God, so we live by grace. We do not live by legalism. His grace makes us strong when discouragement and suffering come. There are no clever, man-made formulas that work like His grace..

Second, we must pass on the truth we learn. To keep it to ourselves is not right and stifles our own growth. We must ntrust truth to *reliable men* as one trusts a bank with his v. This requires wisdom, for in the average church only eople are teachable. Of the half that want to learn, become "safety deposit boxes" which store share it with others. Spiritual multiplication who share truth with others.

ree careers to illustrate a leader's life. ("suffer ill treatment") as a *soldier* ht in wars. God didn't start the et. Satan started it with his rebellion one side or the other. It is no private

116

war, but is much bigger than ourselves. Good soldiers are single-minded, disciplined and obedient. They obey promptly and completely. They never become entangled in worldly affairs unrelated to their calling. No soldier would say, "Sir, I cannot get to the battlefield today. I have a date with a girl (or guy). Then I have a business deal in town." Serving Christ is our business! We aren't working through a playground, but a mine-filled battlefield! We must work to earn a living, but our main aim in life is not to make money. We must hold this world and its "stuff" lightly.

Athletics was one of Paul's favorite topics. He said we must compete as an *runner* in the race of life (Philippians 3:14). This race requires bodily discipline (1 Corinthians 9:24-27). God's Word gives the training rules and He calls all fouls! The race is won through self control, persistence, mental toughness, and purity. Spiritual, not carnal weapons are the only ones which work against Satan (2 Corinthians 10:4). Half-heartedness won't get it done.

Finally, we must work hard as a *farmer* labors over his crops. And we should share in the crop, as a farmer eats his own produce. As we sow the seed of God's Word in hearts and minds, we are encouraged by that Word. We expect God's blessing on our labor as we wait patiently for the crop to mature!

Paul was gratified to write about suffering, endurance, discipline, and hard work. He was chained in a Roman prison for his determined and sustained preaching about Jesus and the resurrection. But he knew the gospel was worth suffering for and he is now enjoying a great reward.

Read 2 Timothy 2:8-13

A Leader's Memory

Remember, Jesus Christ raised from the dead, descended from David.

2 Timothy 2:8

IN KUALA LAMPUR, MALAYSIA, a seven-mile cross-country race was held. Two hours after the race had begun, none of the runners had returned. The officials, fearing that something might have happened, set out in cars to find the runners.

The officials found all of the runners six miles away, and sprinting in the wrong direction. They had forgotten the right way! Many of the runners had already covered distances of ten miles. A. J. Rogers, the association secretary, said the mix-up apparently occurred when the lead runner took a wrong turn at the fifth check point and the rest followed him!

A Christian leader must have a good memory of the right direction, for moral failure begins with memory failure! He must remember that Jesus Christ, who rose from the dead, is coming back to rule as King on David's throne! Sometimes even Christian workers forget their Savior as they do His work! If Paul hadn't kept Jesus at the top of his mind and if he hadn't endured suffering for Him, the gospel would not have gone forward. Paul knew his Master Coach had reasons for all suffering He allowed. Though Paul was chained, God's Word was not restricted. Lenski says, "The apostles' living voice may be smothered in his own blood, but what his Lord speaks through him still resounds in the wide world."

Paul cites an ancient devotional hymn to help us remember Jesus and His gospel:

> "If we died with him,
>   we will also live with him;
> If we endure,
>   we will also reign with him.
> If we disown him,
>   he will also disown us;

If we are faithless,
    he will remain faithful,
    for he cannot disown himself."

If we died with Him, we will also live with Him. Our old self died when we received Him as Savior (Romans 6). We are mystically identified with His death *and* with His resurrected life! Now, we must count ourselves dead to sin, self, and legalistic righteousness. His life is our life! Moreover, if we are physically martyred we will be with Him! In other words, we are known by the company we keep!

If we endure, we will also reign with Him. All who live godly lives will suffer in some way (3:12). Fox says five million were martyred in Paul's day alone. The twentieth century has seen more Christian martyrs than any century of history. Sometimes Christians suffer more criticism for talking about Jesus than they did when they were drinking, cursing, using drugs and sexually abusing others before they were saved! This world is not friendly to Christ's ones. But we are promised to reign with Him!

If we disown Him, he will also disown us. Apostates (those who profess but do not possess Christ) eventually disown Jesus (1 John 2:19). There will be no hypocrites in heaven. No true believer will disown Him in permanent, habitual denial. This refers to a permanent attitude, not a temporary lapse (a la Peter). Real faith always is accompanied by works and by words (James 2:14-26).

If we are faithless, He will remain faithful, for He cannot deny Himself. Peter temporarily denied Jesus, was ashamed, and repented with bitter tears of remorse. Jesus remained faithful to him and used him greatly. Jesus is faithful to His promise never to leave or forsake His believing ones. His faithfulness endures (Psalm 100:5) and He remains eternally loyal (Romans 3:3).

What a leader we follow! What a Savior to remember! If we would lead others, we must keep Him in first place in our minds and memories.

Read 2 Timothy 2:14-26

How a Leader Handles Errors

Do your best to present yourself to God as one approved, a workman who does not need to be ashamed and who correctly handles the word of truth.

2 Timothy 2:15

PHIL LUCKETT IS AN NFL referee who responded correctly to an error and was wrongly blamed for it. In 1998, Phil flipped a coin prior to a Steeler football game. Captain Jerome Bettis called, "Hea . . .uh . . . tails" and Phil correctly went with the first pick. He was widely ridiculed for blowing a coin toss when he made the right decision all along.

When errors are made in the game of life, a good leader must react in the right way. There are a great many errors being committed today! Many people are falling away from the absolute truth of God! How does a leader react?

A good leader *reminds* believers of the truth without quarreling over words. Religious debates turn believers off and accomplish nothing. Stand for sound doctrine, but avoid quibbling.

As good "workmen" (laborers), we must win God's approval by *correctly handling* ("cutting straight") His word of truth. Paul was a tentmaker. We are to "cut straight" God's Word as he cut the canvas straight before sewing it together. Scripture has only one interpretation but many applications. Good leaders correctly interpret and apply God's Word.

A good leader avoids godless chatter. Some religious people speak with empty discourses or "fluff" instead of serious, helpful truth. They are all form and no substance. This leads to error which spreads like cancer (gangrene). Error leads to ungodly living. Some people are advancing steadily down the wrong road. Their false religious systems never remain static. As new dogmas and pronouncements are added, more ungodliness results. Hymanaeus and Philetus were examples. They embraced false teaching concerning bodily resurrection, the cornerstone of Christianity! Perhaps they taught that spiritually accepting Jesus was the only resurrection we would experience. Such a view would stop the church from looking for His return and cause it to settle into this present evil world system. But Jesus is coming back and we will bodily arise to meet Him! False teaching detracts from God's glory! It originates with Satan!

Good leaders remember that whatever God does (His foundation) remains firm and we need not fear the future. As ancient temples were inscribed with a purpose statement (seal), God has sealed us with a truth (He knows and keeps His people) and a command (we must leave sin). God's people depart from sin so they never hear Jesus say, "Depart from me. I never knew you!" Today, Christianity has become a "large house," full of both the saved and those claiming to be saved. Those who know Christ are gold and silver. Those who are deceived are wood and clay. We must recognize this and avoid error in teaching, not leaving the church but forsaking false teaching.

A good leader flees evil desires of youth. Lust for money, power, fame, and pleasure
must not hold him captive. Instead, he pursues righteousness (moral character), faith in God, love for others, and peace.

A good leader avoids foolish arguments. Heretical Jewish teachers argued over senseless genealogies and traditions. Timothy must avoid these. His demeanor in handling error must be forbearing (gentle) to those who antagonized him. He must be able and ready to teach, them, not resentful when hurt. Tact is essential.

Lost people commit many errors. They are like drunks ensnared by Satan as his "prisoners of war." Horton says, "The devil's method of taking men captive is to benumb the conscience, confuse the senses, and paralyze the will." Leaders must gently instruct, hoping that God will bring them to repentance. It's a tall order that can be fulfilled only by the grace of God.

Read 2 Timothy 3:1-9

Opposition to the Leader

— having a form of godliness, but denying its power.
2 Timothy 3:5

FORMER NORTHWESTERN BASKETBALL COACH Ricky Birdsong was a great leader at home and spoke frequently about racial reconciliation within his church. He had written a mission statement for his three children concerning gratitude, giving 100 per cent effort, courage to say "no" to vices, rejecting any philosophy contrary to Scripture, and treating others as they would like to be treated. On July 2, 1999, Ricky was walking with his children outside of Chicago when a racist, who was out to kill African-Americans and Jews, gunned him down. His death revealed the opposition to the good things for which he stood.

The "last days" of the church on earth began shortly after its first days! Paul warned Timothy (and us) of terrible times in the last days of the church. These are times of intensified difficulty when it is hard to endure. They are times of low moral character, opposition to anything good, and a breakdown of law and tradition. The most severe opposition to real Christians comes from those who claim to be religious! They regard Christianity as a philosophy instead of a relationship with Jesus, denying that God intervenes in the affairs of men.

Paul lists nineteen traits of people living in the last days. Every one is prominent among athletes and the general public today! They are *"self-lovers,"* drawing attention to themselves after every tackle or basket, craving media coverage and pats on the back. Many people are "self-made" men who worship their creator! They l*ove money*, desiring more than the next guy as a measure of their worth. They are *boastful.* "The swagger is back" is stated as a proud boast as men forsake humility. They are *proud, abusive* and *disobedient to parents*. When children never learn to obey parents, it is unlikely they will obey any authority, including God. They are *unthankful, unholy* and *without real love* ("natural affection"). Parents aren't loving children today. Natural affection is replaced by

122

unnatural affection (homosexuality). McGee says, "Humanity sinks to its lowest level when it accepts homosexuality." They are *unforgiving* and idolize it. There is even a band named "Unforgiven." They are *slanderers*, like the devil whose name means "accuser." They lack *self-control*, which characterizes our obese, drunken, addicted and promiscuous society. They are *brutal*, turning the streets into a jungle. They *don't love good* but glorify evil, are *treacherous*, rash (not caring about consequences), *conceited* know-it-alls, and *lovers of pleasure* who spend billions on pleasure, just like the first century Romans who cried, "Give us bread and the circus." Today, their cry is "Give us welfare and entertainment."

Finally, they have religion but no power. Paul said, "turn away from them." Don't go to a dead church! Many are dead today, lacking power because of sin. God is not committed or obeyed on the issues of life. We have a new paganism which masquerades as Christianity in church!

The traitors on the inside who oppose the gospel use the same tactic as Satan used on Eve. They attack women when their husbands are away, playing heavily on their gullibility. First century Gnosticism and today's cults are similar. These false teachers resemble Jannes and Jambres, the Egyptian magicians who opposed Moses by imitating God's miracles through Satan's power (Exodus 7:11, 22). Ancient Jewish literature mentions their names. But the gospel will triumph over opposition just as God's truth prevailed in Egypt. The folly of traitors becomes clear when they must answer the question, "Is Jesus Christ God?" Faith healers and other deceivers soon fade away leaving disillusioned followers. Don't be tricked by a traitor — even if he is within a church!

Read 2 Timothy 3:10-17

A Leader's Supply Line

All Scripture is God-breathed and is useful for teaching, rebuk-
ing, correcting and training in righteousness, so that the man of
God may be thoroughly equipped for every good work.
                                                    2 Timothy 3:16-17

NO GOOD LEADER is ever cut off from his line of supply. For
a military leader to run out of ammunition, gasoline, food, or
water spells defeat. For a coach to run out of players means a
season of losses. For the athlete to not consume a balanced
diet means subpar performances.

Paul's supply line for giving out the gospel was the Word of
God. He never got cut off from this supply line and he wanted
Timothy to remember that principle. Correct teaching (not his
experience) was the foundation of his walk with God. The very
tone of Paul's life, his purpose, faith, love, patience, and his
sufferings confirmed his teaching. Timothy remembered how
the Jews had run Paul out of Antioch (Acts 13), Iconium, and
Lystra, where he was stoned and left for dead (Acts 14). Only
God had spared his life and Timothy knew it.

Paul said all true believers would suffer because we live in
a dying world which is basically opposed to Jesus, the only
Hope of eternal life. Naturally, Christians will be persecuted in
school, on the job, and even in some churches. Paul says it
will get worse. Why? A godly life exposes the sin of sinners.
Instead of repenting, many seek to destroy the ones who
expose them for what they are. The Columbine High School
and Wedgewood Baptist Church shootings demonstrate that it
is becoming increasingly dangerous to be a Christian in
America. Christianity condemns all religions, some of them
very ancient. Christianity denies the basic goodness of mankind, which is a foundational lie in America. Christianity
promises no immediate self-gratification. We await a permanent home in heaven. The cross of Christ is a stumbling block
over which multitudes fall. The irony is that deceivers who
teach otherwise (apostates) are the deceived ones! Sin feeds
upon itself and grows like cancerous cells. It is progressively

124

malignant and hostile to anything good. The more scientific our discoveries, the more grievous our sins! We invent television and the internet, so we broadcast pornography. We advance in medicine, so we kill millions of unborn babies. We make chemical discoveries, so we exterminate people like rats.

Timothy was fortunate to have been taught the Old Testament when he was a child. Others probably said he was following old-fashioned ideas or that he was "anti-intellectual" or "unscientific." But Paul says that all Scripture is inspired ("God-breathed"). Peter says all Scripture came from the Holy Spirit (2 Peter 1:21). God's Word produces faith (Romans 10:17) and faith in Christ leads to salvation from sin (Ephesians 2:8-9). Salvation is not found by doing good works, baptism, church membership, sacraments, confirmation, or anything man does. Scripture is the road map to heaven pointing to the cross and the finished work of Christ. Scripture is useful for *teaching* what to believe and do, for *rebuking* sin, for *correcting* our errors, and for *training* how to go on. In other words, Scripture shows the path of life to walk on, where we've gotten off that path, how to return to the path, and how to stay on the path. Scripture, not tradition or church policy, is our authority.

Every original word of Scripture is inspired by God and our translations are very reliable. First Corinthians 2:13 says, "This is what we speak, not in words taught us by human wisdom, but in words taught by the Spirit, expressing spiritual truths in spiritual words." Jesus said every word and even the original punctuation was important (Matthew 5:18). God's men were moved by the Holy Spirit to record God's Word (2 Peter 1:20-21). In 1 Timothy 5:18, Paul quotes Luke as Scripture. Second Peter 3:16 speaks of Paul's letters as Scripture. The Jews took God's Old Testament inspiration for granted, but Paul, Peter, and others confirm the inspiration of the New Testament also. These leaders knew where their supply of strength came from and they never got cut off from it. Neither should we!

The Best Strategy

Preach the word; be prepared in season and out of season; correct, rebuke, and encourage — with great patience and careful instruction.

2 Timothy 4:2

THE CINCINNATI BENGALS once lost a game to San Francisco because of poor strategy. On November 18, 1987, the Bengals led 27-21 and had the ball on their own 25-yard line. San Francisco was out of time-outs, but rather than punt, the Bengals went for a first down on fourth down, failed, and the 49ers took over with two seconds left. Joe Montana fired a TD pass to Jerry Rice on the final play and the Bengals lost!

Christians must use better strategy than the Bengals used against the 49ers. Paul has said that Scripture "thoroughly equips for every good work." He reminds us that Jesus Christ will judge our service, He will establish His kingdom, and faithful ones will be given authority (Luke 19:11-27). It is pointless to be equipped and then sit down on the bench and do nothing about it. In light of our accountability to the Master Coach, Paul relays a "game plan" to Timothy. These orders apply to all Christians, whether our calling is as clergy or as coaches, whether our platform is in school or on the street. We are to *preach the Word* of God. We must do it when it is convenient (in season) and when it is not (out of season). We must *take* the opportunity or *make* the opportunity! There is an urgency to get God's Word to people, for our time is limited. We are not called to give our opinions, to give the ideas of our mistaken culture, to repeat popular opinions, or to spout philosophical jargon. We are not to preach *about* the Word or *from* the Word (taking verses out of context), but to preach the Word itself! Timothy was told to correct error, rebuke sin, and encourage right living with great patience and careful instruction.

Paul warned that a time was coming when people wouldn't tolerate sound ("healthy") teaching. Senaca said, "Some come to *hear*, not to *learn*, just as we go to the theatre, for pleasure,

to delight our ears with the speaking or the voice of the plays."
This had also happened in Isaiah's day (Isaiah 30:9-11), and
seems to be the case today. Many want to be entertained by
Christian performers. Some don't want what is good for them,
but only what satisfied their sinful desires and keeps their
pride intact. People today will tolerate any devious, perverted
sin but shun truth. One cannot criticize any group or religion
in our "politically correct" society — except Biblical Christianity. Only Christians who profess the absolutes of Scripture
can be scorned today. Man has turned from truth to myths.

Paul advised Timothy not to panic when he saw the
church flooded with error. "Keep your head in all situations,"
he said. Literally the phrase is, "abstain from intoxicating
drinks." He must endure hardship, continue to share the
gospel, and do all God called him to do.

Hiebert says Paul had one foot in the grave and his heart
in heaven. He knew he was soon to depart this earth like a
ship leaving the dock for the open sea. He was soon taken to
the death chamber and his head laid on a chopping block.
Then a Roman soldier took a sharp ax and severed it with one
stroke. But Paul was ready. He finished strong. He had
"fought the good fight" of defending the Word of God. He had
finished his part of the race and was passing the baton to
Timothy and to us. He had kept the faith and he looked
forward to his reward.

In the Old Testament, wine was poured on the hot, brazen
altar while it was consuming the animal sacrifice. This "drink
offering" would go up as steam. Paul was going to pour out
his life as a drink offering on the sacrifice of Christ. All that
could be seen was Christ! He didn't want a building or a
church pew named for him. He only wanted Jesus to be
exalted. He had reached the end of life and had no regrets
with how he had invested it for Christ. By following his "game
plan," we can do the same!

Read 2 Timothy 4:9-22

Loyalty to a Leader

Do your best to come to me quickly . . .

2 Timothy 4:9

IN 1992, RELIEF ACE DENNIS ECKERSLEY signed a two-year deal with Oakland when he could have received much more money from another team. But the A's had given Dennis his first chance at baseball — and his second chance after a battle with alcoholism. Loyalty took precedence over money, a rare occurrence in the world of most pro sports of the 1990s.

Loyalty was sometimes hard to find in Rome during the 60s AD, and it was very dangerous to be a Christian. It was even more dangerous to identify with Paul. The emperor Nero had burned his own city, blamed the Christians, outlawed Christianity, and arrested Paul. Though his first trial was continued (v 17), Paul knew his eventual outcome would be execution. Unlike most Christians, it was not at the mouths of the lions, but by beheading as a Roman citizen.

Paul's last known written words were from the Mamertine Prison. Cold and lonely, he desired to see Timothy one last time. Knowing the loyalty of his "son" in the faith, Paul asked him to come many miles to see him before winter and to bring his heavy poncho, his scrolls and his parchments. Paul intended to study and to write until death! Old leaders have some loyal followers and some who are disloyal. Paul mentioned many people of both kinds.

Dr. Luke, one of God's most humble servants, also remained loyal to Paul. Others had gone their separate ways. Demas has started strong, had served with Paul (Colossians 4:14, Philemon 24), but then he fell in love with the present world. He stopped looking for Jesus' appearing, and left Paul. Paul felt the disappointment of broken fellowship with a former friend. Yet, he wasn't bitter. Crescens ("growing") had gone to Galatia and Titus to Dalmatia (Yugoslavia), probably to share Christ. Mark, who had deserted Paul in the past, was forgiven and he matured. Paul's confidence in him was restored and he wanted to see him before he died. Tychicus probably carried this letter to Timothy in Ephesus.

128

Alexander was hostile to Paul's message and may have brought false charges against him, leading to his imprisonment. Maybe he was charged with treason because of refusing to sacrifice to the Roman gods or to worship the Emperor. Paul warned Timothy to beware of him. God (not Paul) would repay Alexander for his deeds (Romans 12:19). Paul refused to become bitter.

Priscilla, Aquila, Onesiphorous, and Erastus (city treasurer of Corinth) had been loyal friends of Paul. Trophimus was an Ephesian whom Paul had left in Miletus. No details are given. We know Paul did healing miracles to confirm the gospel as God allowed, but not for personal convenience. If it was God's will, Paul could have healed Trophemus. Eubulus, Pudens, Linus (who succeeded Peter as bishop of Rome) and Claudia were Roman Christians who may have been driven underground.

Paul praised God in the face of death (v 18). He had long ago discounted his own life for the gospel's sake (Acts 20:24). He was delivered from the evil of denying Jesus' name, of recanting his witness, and from moral breakdown. He was destined for heaven and the ax of the executioner would send him there!

TITUS
Introduction

ANY GOOD LEADER IS CONCERNED about the organization of his followers, for we always achieve more when we work together in harmony. The apostle Paul was a good leader. While on his way to Nicopolis around 64 AD, he wrote an organizational letter to Titus, pastor on the pagan island of Crete. According to Homer, there were 90 to 100 cities on Crete. Organization of churches (Chapter 1), sound teaching (Chapter 2), and good works (Chapter 3) are the themes of the letter.

Titus was one of Paul's Gentile converts (Galatians 2:3). He became an enthusiastic peer of Paul and represented him in Corinth (2 Corinthians 2, 7, 8). Crete was the mythical birthplace of the false god Zeus and of Minotaur, a half-bull, half-man monster for which King Minos secured slaves as food. Paul directed Titus to go to every town on the island to straighten out the difficulties in the churches. Though the gospel was widespread on Crete, Satan had tried to overthrow the churches' organization and to corrupt sound doctrine with lies. Paul's letter would give Titus increased credibility and authority. Today, Titus is regarded as "patron saint" of Crete.

Paul's emphasis was not upon building great buildings, but upon building great people by the power of the gospel. He was concerned about doing good works and helping others to do the same. All who understand the grace of God cannot help but be concerned about doing good works (Titus 3:8). May we be among them!

Read Titus 1:1-4

The Motivation of Paul

Paul, a servant of God and an apostle of Jesus Christ for the faith of God's elect and the knowledge of the truth that leads to godliness —

Titus 1:1

PAT RILEY IS KNOWN as a master motivator. He has used a variety of ploys to inspire teams. Once he gave a speech to his Miami Heat team about a coach who dunked one of his players in a bucket of ice water for almost a minute before finally lifting his head out of the water.

"You will win when winning is as important as that next breath," he said to the team.

The apostle Paul was highly motivated and he began his letter to Titus by giving both his titles and his motivation. His title is servant ("bond slave") of God, which means he has chosen to be a slave for life though given his freedom. His title of apostle means he was given authority to tell Titus how to organize churches. He was an apostle not by his choice, but by God's choice.

The motivation of Paul was the faith of Christians (God's elect). He wanted to build their faith. All Christians are elected by God and would recognize truth taught by Paul and Titus, as they opposed the heresy of false teachers. Paul's second motivation was the education of believers through preaching. Knowledge of truth would increase the faith of believers. Both faith and knowledge rest upon the hope of eternal life. The word "hope" does not imply any uncertainty, however. Believers in Jesus have a sure thing. We have a *guarantee* of eternal life! God cannot lie and He made a promise before He created the world. The promise was made to His Son, Jesus. God promised to save all sinners who put their faith in His Son (3:5-7)! This eternal plan, kept hidden for centuries was now being brought to light!

Today, many Christians do not study God's Word. They become "experience oriented" and base their beliefs upon feelings rather than objective truth. Experience and feelings can be very deceitful! Only God's Word is consistently reliable. We are to take His truth and act upon it.

Paul wishes grace and peace to pastor Titus. Grace provides "divine strength" for his job. Peace means "freedom from anxiety despite adversity." There were problems in churches. There were problems outside of churches. Faith and knowledge, based upon the certainty of eternal life, would overcome them all.

Read Titus 1:5-9

Qualifications to Lead

An elder must be . . .

Titus 1:6

JONATHAN EDWARDS was a great leader and a great preacher. He would have been a valuable asset to the elders on Crete. Edwards resolved:

> To live with all my might while I do life;
> Never to lose one moment of time;
> Never to do anything which I should despise or think meanly of in another;
> Never to do anything out of revenge;
> Never to do anything which I should be afraid to do if it were the last hour of my life.

All was not well among believers on the island of Crete, one of the largest islands in the Mediterranean Sea. Cretans who had been at Jerusalem during Pentecost (Acts 2:5, 11) must have brought the faith home with them, but they needed organization. Titus' job was to appoint leaders in every town where there was a group of believers. This was essential, with so much false teaching circulating among the churches. Paul gives the scriptural plan for several elders ("bishops" or "guardians") with authority to watch over the "flock of God" without "fleecing" the flock!

Titus did not have dictatorial powers to appoint leaders, for there were qualifications they must meet. First, church leaders must be men. Women may teach groups of children and other women, but they are never to lead, teach, or administer over men in the plan of God. Paul gives the order of creation and the deception of Eve as God's reasons (1 Timothy 2). Women were allowed to be deaconesses ("servants"), whose role differs from elders.

Second, an elder must be blameless. What does this mean? It doesn't mean "sinless" or none could lead! "Blameless" means not blamable because he continually confesses sin and is covered by the blood of Jesus.

Next, a leader must not be overbearing. Loud, domineering people are disqualified. Most overbearing people don't realize they are overbearing. Also, he must not be quick-tempered. They must not be "touchy," but slow to anger (Proverbs 14:29, 19:11).

A leader must not be a drunkard. Drunkards tell the whole world they are unsaved (Galatians 5:19-21, 1 Corinthians 6:9-11). Leaders must not be violent. Righteous anger can be released in constructive ways. Anger with sin must be properly channeled.

A leader must not be a crook! He must feed, not milk the flock of God! Stipends associated with ministry were attractive in those days. Preachers preaching for the money were preaching for the wrong reason. All these vices were common among Greeks of the first century.

The family of a church leader is important, for it affirms or denies his ability to lead in a Godly way. He must have one wife. Any group advocating polygamy (Mormonism) is disobeying God. His children must believe. They must not be "wild" and disobedient. Any man who cannot control his family cannot direct God's family (1 Timothy 3:5). Church leaders had to make judgments about others. Members could point fingers if the leader's own children were rebellious. Therefore, rebellious children disqualified leaders from leadership in the church.

Leaders must be hospitable. Traveling evangelists needed temporary housing, and leaders needed to provide it joyfully. Also, some Christians were kicked out of their homes when they accepted Jesus. They had no other place to go.

Leaders must love the good, be self-controlled (empowered by the Holy Spirit), upright, holy, and disciplined. Since conflict in the church is inevitable, the leaders must be theologically sound. They must teach others and refute false teaching. Doctrinal error is seldom an innocent mistake. Some degree of culpability is usually involved. Paul never hesitated to point it out (Acts 13:6-10).

Leading God's people is even more important than leading a football team. The qualifications are many. Nothing is mentioned about physical strength, business acumen, education or social status, but the qualities mentioned are indispensable.

Read Titus 1:10-16

"Liar, Liar . . ."

They must be silenced, because they are ruining whole households by teaching things they ought not to teach — and that for the sake of dishonest gain.

Titus 1:11

IN 1999, IT WAS REVEALED that both Boston newspapers — the Herald and the Globe — had been printing phony high school hockey scores for thirty years! A "gentlemen's agreement" existed among coaches, who called in results. They toned down final scores of lopsided games. For example, instead of a 10-1 true score, the reported score might be 5-4. The lies continued and evidently no one complained.

In the early church, men had freedom to speak publicly as "led by the Spirit" (1 Corinthians 14:26). But, because of their sin nature, men with false doctrines and endless ramblings devoid of the spirit soon took over. The need for elders arose because of these false teachers.

Cretans had a bad reputation in general. In BC 600, a poet named Epimenides had referred to Cretans as liars, evil brutes, and lazy gluttons. Paul said this statement was true, even though it was stated by a Cretan! In fact, to "Cretanize" came to mean "to lie."

Not only was lying generally accepted on Crete, but people were cruel and rude. They were addicted to food and allergic to work. They were called "slow bellies" and they lived for their stomachs. Like many Americans, a main topic of their conversation was where and what they ate!

Josephus says many Cretans were Jewish. They professed Christianity but insisted on their ceremonial laws. This led to Gnosticism, as it appealed to the legalistic nature in man (Colossians 2:23). They were full of hot air. Their much talk had little substance. These empty talkers found gullible people to *pay them* for their false teaching. These false teachers must have resembled some today with elaborate TV ministries! Not all TV preachers are false teachers, but several are all glitter and no substance. Paul says these teachers must be sharply rebuked and there was no time to lose. They had gone door to door disrupting entire households.

Paul's point in verse 15 has often been taken out of context and used to justify every behavior. Sins are sinful no matter who does them! But Christians (pure) need not call some foods clean and some unclean. Judaism taught such legalism (Mark 7:18-19). Unbelievers (Jewish false teachers) were entirely corrupt and yet tried to attach themselves to the church of Christ. Nothing they could eat would make them pure. Their minds were unclean and defiled. Only faith in Christ could purify them.

To whom are you listening? How do you react to false teaching? Sometimes a rebuke is in order. Love never glosses over sin or false teaching. We must stand for truth, no matter who we must stand against!

Read Titus 2:1-10

Dress Up the Truth

You must teach what is in accord with sound doctrine.

Titus 2:1

. . . so that in every way they will make the teaching about God our Savior attractive.

Titus 2:10

PHIL DAWSON WALKED WITH GOD as a place-kicker for the Texas Longhorns. In the spring of 1995, Playboy magazine selected him to their pre-season All-America team. But the courage of his convictions to stand for Christ and against what Playboy represents led Phil to refuse the honor. "I found total peace with the decision," he explained. "Many people respected my decision, but some didn't understand taking Playboy's offer was not right for me with what I am trying to do with my life.

Sound doctrine (teaching) is the foundation of right living. Sound doctrine refuted the false teachers that threatened the churches on Crete. Sound teaching is intensely practical and practice must be intensely doctrinal. Paul says we are to "adorn" or "dress up" sound doctrine with right living. By so doing, we make the truth look good to others. In fact, we make God look good to others. Truth is still truth, no matter whether we live it or not. But when it is lived out in practice, it appeals to those in darkness. Phil Dawson lived out the truth and in doing so, he "dressed it up!"

A good teacher of truth cannot be afraid to be different. Otherwise, how can he benefit his learners? Indeed, he must be different from those in error and from those who are uninformed! Remember, Cretans were liars, evil brutes and lazy gluttons. Titus must go against that lifestyle. Paul writes specific instructions for various members of God's team. First, older men are to be stable influences. They are to be worthy of respect. They must not be dirty old men or shallow thinkers, but must be self-controlled. They must be optimistic and fun to be around. They are to be sound in faith, love, and endur-ance. When concrete is poured, it must be poured into the right frame. When men are formed, if they are formed in sound doctrine, they will hold the church together over time. Old age does not automatically mean Christian maturity. Some men who are saved later in life have bad habit patterns that must be broken. There are more sins on their con-sciences. Remember, when Jesus challenged "those who are without sin to cast the first stone" at the adulterous woman, the oldest religious leader was the first to depart (John 8:7-9)!

Older women may have more time because their children are gone from the home. Titus was to teach them to be rever-ent ("purposeful"), not to slander others, to avoid addiction to wine (1 Corinthians 6:10-11), and to teach what is good. Such older women could teach younger women. Titus was not told to teach young women. More older women should be teaching young women today! They should especially train them to love their husbands and children. These young housewives have the world's most vital jobs. It is said that the hand that rocks the cradle rules the world! The young women should be self-controlled ("sensible"), pure ("chaste"), busy at home ("domestic"), kind and subject ("subordinate" or "responsive to") their husbands. If they live these kind of lives, God's Word cannot be honestly maligned. They will "adorn the truth" by their lifestyles.

Paul knew Titus could not order or merely suggest proper conduct to young men. He was to encourage them ("persuade on the basis of God's Word") to be self-controlled. Titus must model such behavior by doing good. He must show integrity in teaching by giving the entire message in balance and without distortion. His seriousness and sound speech would give no ammunition for slander to Satan or to ungodly men. Young men can follow God. Daniel did so while a captive in a foreign land. Young Samuel heard God speak. Josiah walked uprightly at age 8. Timothy knew Scripture while a child and Jesus confounded His elders at age 12.

There were multitudes of slaves under the Roman empire in Paul's day. Ninety percent of names on the walls of the catacombs are those of slaves or ex-slaves! Paul said slaves were to be subject to masters in everything. He didn't say "form a union and go on strike," but to obey bosses (Ephesians 6:5-8). Many masters were won to Christ by their slaves' behavior! Slaves (employees) are not to talk back to bosses, nor to steal from them (Businesses lose millions of dollars to employee theft each year.). By being trustworthy, Christian employees "dress up" the gospel.

Believers must apply "Christian Cosmetics" to their faith by their behavior. Good behavior adorns the gospel. When Christians fail to dress up God's Word with their actions, the Word of God is blasphemed (v 5) by the unbelievers. Are you dressing up the gospel by your attitudes and actions?

Read Titus 2:11-15

Grace in Three Time Zones

For the grace of God that brings salvation has appeared to all men.

Titus 2:11

PRO TEAMS MUST ADJUST to large amounts of travel across America. In such travel, multiple time zones are involved. Flying at high rates of speed across the country, it is sometimes possible to arrive at a destination before they leaving the point of origin! The "jet lag" across time zones is a factor that must be overcome if teams are to play their best.

God appears in all three "time zones" of human existence, but He certainly experiences no jet lag! In the past, God showed His grace in Jesus. 2 Corinthians 8:9 says, "For you know the grace of our Lord Jesus Christ, that though he was rich, yet for your sakes he became poor, so that you through his poverty might become rich." The Creator of the Universe (John 1:3) took our sins upon Himself (Romans 8:16). God didn't save us by His love, for His justice makes His love powerless by itself. He didn't save us by His mercy, for if that were the case all men would be saved! He saved us by His grace (Ephesians 2:8-9). GRACE is God's Riches At Christ's Expense. His grace is undeserved and unsolicited. It is His idea alone. Now, He asks only that we trust in Christ to be saved. His way is not only the best way, it is the *only* way to be saved! His grace is available to all, but is rejected by most.

In the present time zone, God's grace teaches ("child trains") us to deny ungodliness and worldly passions. Grace is a better teacher than law. We can "just say no" to ungodly deeds by grace. Those who have experienced His grace want to do right! Their direction is changed from worldly lusts to godly living. Anyone claiming to know God will walk as He walked. Those who live otherwise haven't experienced grace and don't really know God (1 John 2:3-6).

139

The next time zone on God's calendar is the coming of Jesus Christ (2 Thessalonians 4:14-17). What a great hope for the future we have (1 Corinthians 15:19)! This hope is not the idea of "maybe it will happen," but a certainty. He has "redeemed" us from the curse of the law! Though we were slaves of sin, He has purchased us, removed us from the marketplace, and set us free! Our hope of heaven is going to be fulfilled as surely as any other promise of God. While we wait for Him, we must be eager ("zealous" or "passionate") to do good works. It is the passionate people who change the world.

Paul told Titus to teach these facts with authority. He must encourage others and rebuke error. Jesus did so. So should we.

Read Titus 3:1-2

Relationships with Others

Remind the people to be subject to rulers and authorities, to be obedient, to be ready to do whatever is good, to slander no one, to be peaceable and considerate and to show true humility toward all men.

Titus 3:1-2

THE U.S. TOURING TABLE TENNIS TEAM was unexpectedly invited to communist China on April 7, 1971. The fifteen players became the first American group into China since the mid-50s. Their visit led to political discussion between the two countries. A relationship developed because of what was termed "Ping-Pong Diplomacy."

Lasting relationships with others depend upon far more than "Ping-Pong Diplomacy." The grace of God is the "root" of all good relationships with others. Good works are the "fruit." Paul's theme in Titus chapter 3 is that we must do what is good in our relationships with others. He begins by talking about the Christian's relationship to government.

Crete had been a democracy until BC 67. At that time, the Romans under Metellus conquered the island. For 125 years Crete had been under the government of the Roman Empire. Diodorus Siculus mentions their insubordination. Paul says

Christians ought to be submissive to rulers (magistrates) and authorities. An imperfect government is better than no government, which would lead to anarchy. As long as an authority doesn't command us to violate God's revealed will, we must obey the laws of the land. Generally, the aim of government is to reward the good and to punish evil.

We must be careful not to speak evil of anyone. Lasting relationships depend upon our words. To "slander" means to utter or spread false statements harmful to another person's character or reputation. Slander was very Cretan and is very American today. Christians must avoid slander. Yet, naming obvious sins of evil men is not slander. Paul named several men in his letters who had done wrong deeds.

Lasting relationships depend upon peace, consideration and humility. We must esteem others better than ourselves (Philippians 2:3), not insisting upon our "rights." We lost our rights to have our own way when we came to the cross! Now, we want things His way! A wise man has written that there are two jobs in this world. One is to be humble and the other is to be exalted. Our job is to humble ourselves and God's job is to exalt us. When we do our job, God does His job! But if we insist upon doing God's job, He'll do ours! Humble yourselves before the Lord, and He will lift you up (James 4:10). Our relationships depend upon it.

Read Titus 3:3-8

When Good Works Count

This is a trustworthy saying. And I want you to stress these things, so that those who have trusted in God may be careful to devote themselves to doing what is good.

Titus 3:8

LATE IN THE FOURTH QUARTER, a fleet running back darted and dodged 50-yards through the defense for an apparent game-winning touchdown. Fans celebrated on the home side! But back up field, a red flag marked the site of a holding penalty. The score was nullified, the crowd quieted, and the game was lost.

The forward took the pass in the corner and drove the baseline. He knifed underneath the outstretched arms of the fallen defender and laid the basketball neatly off the glass and into the hole! But the shrill whistle of a referee silenced the crowd's roar of approval. The forward had stepped on the end line and the basket was no good.

Sometimes a great play counts for a score. And sometimes, because a rule is violated, it doesn't. Sometimes good works count before God. And sometimes they are filthy rags. What makes the difference? The difference is the motive. The difference is the power behind the works. Works done to earn salvation mean nothing because salvation is a gift of God to everyone who simply believes in Jesus. Likewise for works done in human strength. They too are worthless.

During the Victorian Era, people tried to cover over the terrible evils in society. Today, the base nature of mankind is broadcast on television and sold in the newspaper! Civilization is a thin veneer covering the savagery of man. What a tragedy to be lost in sin! All of us have been lost or are still lost! When Paul says we were foolish, he means we were "lacking in understanding." First Corinthians 2:14 says, "The man without the Spirit does not accept the things that come from the Spirit of God, for they are foolishness to him, and he cannot understand them, because they are spiritually discerned." When we were lost, we were *led* astray, but we also strayed from God by our *own* choices (Isaiah 53:6). We were deceived about who God is and what God does. Evil movies like "Superstar" and "Godspell" led many to wrong conclusions about the Lord Jesus Christ. Inaccurate ideas cause others to think of God as a mean old man who is opposed to them. Some underestimate His justice or His love. Others are deceived into thinking He is weak, indifferent to their sin, ignorant, or limited. But if we are wrong about God, we will be wrong about man, sin, the world, Satan, and salvation!

Before believing in Jesus, we were enslaved by our own passions and pleasures. The next arousal of our senses and emotions was our great goal in life. We lived in malice (desiring evil upon others) and envy (begrudging good fortune to others). We hated others and they hated us. Our lives were not a pretty picture before knowing Christ. As Duane Litfin says, "Apart from God, people degenerate into little more than animals wrangling over bones."

142

But everything changed when we became saved! We were saved because God is kind (Gr. "philanthropia"), loving, and merciful! If not for the grace of God, we'd still be in our terribly lost condition! We aren't saved by our good works, for they are nothing but filthy rags before God if done in an attempt to merit salvation (Isaiah 64:6). We are saved by grace through faith in Christ, who died on the cross to pay our penalty! We were washed clean by the blood of Jesus (Revelation 1:5). We are washed clean daily by the water of God's Word (John 3:5). The Holy Spirit uses God's Word to cleanse us (Ephesians 5:26). He renews (regenerates) us when we accept Jesus as Savior. He justifies us by His grace. Justification is an accounting term meaning He "counts us as righteous." This happens in the mind of God (Romans 3:26). Justification is for the ungodly (Romans 4:5). Before we are saved, we strangely tried to justify ourselves. Some of us thought we were good people. But in heaven there are *no* people boasting of their goodness! We have a future in heaven only because Jesus is good and His goodness is credited to our account!

After believing in Jesus, our good works become important! They count towards eternal rewards! They confirm that we have been justified. God is very concerned that we represent Him well with good works. He gives us new thoughts, new desires, and new affections. We are to glorify Him by our good works (Matthew 4:16). To glorify means to please Him, to praise Him, to cause others to think well of Him, and to desire Him.

Do your good works count to the glory of God? Or, will they be nullified because you haven't come to Christ for forgiveness and salvation?

Read Titus 3:9-15

Handling Team Problems

Warn a divisive person once, and them warn him a second time. After that, have nothing to do with him.

Titus 3:10

AS LONG AS PEOPLE make up an athletic team, there will be problems to be handled by coaches. Players get into trouble with the law, with their teachers, with the NCAA, with girl-friends, and with agents. No program is immune from problems. The important thing is the way in which the coach and institution handle their problems.

No church is without problems either. Therefore, it is vital that leaders make wise judgments about the disposition of every problem. Paul gave Titus some good advice for handling divisive issues of the day. Disputes about unclean foods, Sabbath regulations, genealogies, and whether to observe certain "holy" days abounded as people who had followed Judaism accepted Jesus as Messiah. But we are told to avoid foolish questions that detract from real issues. Profitless discussions about genealogies, methods of serving communion, or modes of baptism accomplish nothing, even today.

Divisive people are to be warned twice and then dismissed from the team. A divisive person (Gr. "hairetikos") is one who chooses to believe whatever he wants in spite of what God says. He is warped (Gr. "ektrepo," meaning twisted as a sprained ankle"). His attitude is public so he is to be publicly rejected.

Christians are to maintain good works, engaging only in honorable occupations which provide a living. For a Christian to tend bar, engage in prostitution, operate a casino, perform abortions, or own stock in a brewery is not honorable to God.

All of us have problems. Whatever problems arise, we press on through life, handling our assignments by God's grace. He gave grace to Paul and to Titus. He gives the same grace to us as we handle the problems of a new millennium!

PHILEMON
Introduction

PAUL, STILL ON THE "D.L." in a Roman prison (62 AD), wrote a personal letter of appeal to a Christian friend (Philemon) in Colosse. Wealthy Philemon, his wife Apphia, and his son Archippus walked with God. In fact, they hosted a church in their home. This was not uncommon, for there were no church buildings for the first 200 years of Christianity! Paul, who had led Philemon to Christ, had an appeal to make to him.

It seems that Philemon had a slave named Onesimus who had probably robbed him before escaping to Rome. There, Onesimus had met Paul. Onesimus listened to Paul in prison, realized he was still in spiritual bondage, repented of sin, and believed in Jesus! He became free in Christ! He was now a brother to both Paul and Philemon. Since repentance leads to restitution, Paul is sending him back to Philemon.

Does Paul condone slavery? No! But let's examine the situation. In the Roman world, half the population of 120 million people were enslaved to the other half. Slaves were of no particular nationality. Most were from Rome's conquered territories. Many Romans owned ten slaves, but some owned hundreds. Life was not easy for them. They could be beaten for minor offenses and crucified for running away. Paul did not advocate armed rebellion of slaves, for more suffering would have resulted. Paul did encourage earning or buying one's freedom if possible (1 Corinthians 7:20-24). Only when Biblical teaching on man's dignity and value permeated the world was slavery peacefully abolished anywhere on earth. Every ancient civilization practiced slavery but real Christianity has led to freedom. It was a weak hypocrisy which formerly allowed slavery in America.

Old Testament slavery was different. Hebrew servants (Leviticus 25:53) were to be well treated. Some chose sevanthood for life (Exodus 21). Fellow Jews who were servants were to be set free after six years. Some sold themselves to pay debts.

Paul had a request of Philemon. His request was to receive Onesimus as a brother. Tradition says Onesimus later became a bishop in the church. Paul's appeal must have been successful.

145

Read Philemon

Do Right

So if you consider me as a partner, welcome him as you would welcome me. If he has done you any wrong or owes you anything, charge it to me.

Philemon 17-18

TAXI DRIVER AL GUTIEREZ found six Final Four tickets and $10,000 cash in the back seat of his cab in March of 1998. He knew immediately what to do. He returned everything to the owner. "The thought never even crossed my mind to take any of it," said Mr. Gutierez. Everyone I know is calling me a dummy for not taking it all, but I didn't want to. Besides, what kind of example would that set for my children?"

Al Gutierez knew what was right and he did it. Sixty-year-old Paul was a prisoner of Jesus Christ in a Roman prison. He would be released when Jesus, not Rome, said he would be released. But regardless of circumstances, Paul was bound to do what was right and he expected fellow believers to do likewise. So, he appealed to his friend Philemon to receive back Onesimus ("useful") as a brother. Knowing that forced kindness is insincere, he requested Philemon to be graceful.

The basis of Paul's appeal is love. If Christians don't act out of love, their Christianity is hypocritical. The acceptance of Onesimus by Philemon illustrates the gospel itself! Paul seeks *reconciliation* between the two men, just as we have been reconciled to God. Paul sought a welcome for Onesimus as a *substitute* for his own welcome, just as Jesus substituted Himself for us. Paul offered to pay any debt owed by Onesimus, just as Jesus paid our debt by *imputation* of his righteousness to our account!

Going back to his master probably wasn't easy for Onesimus. But it was the right thing to do. The message of Paul is to do right, even if it means hardship. His message still speaks today.

146

Appendix

The Winning Run

PERHAPS YOU HAVE READ this book, but never personally trusted the Savior with your earthly life and your eternal destiny. The following baseball illustration explains how you can come to know the Lord Jesus Christ:

In baseball, a runner must touch all four bases to score a run for his team. The path to abundant and eternal life is very similar to the base paths on a ball diamond.

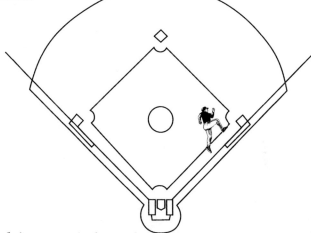

Step 1 (FIRST BASE) along that path is realizing that God cares about you. He not only created you, but He also loves you very deeply. He is seeking to give you an abundant life now and for eternity.

For God so loved the world that He gave His one and only Son, that whoever believes in Him shall not perish but have eternal life.

John 3:16

I have come that they may have life, and have it to the fullest.

147   John 10:10

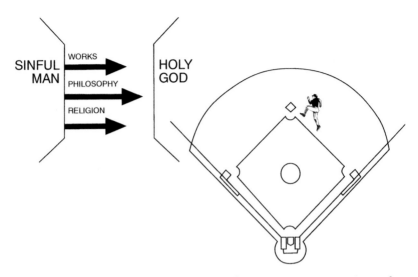

At SECOND BASE (step 2) we admit that we are sinners and separated from God. He is perfect, pure, and good; we are not. Because by nature we disobey Him and resist Him, He cannot have fellowship with us without denying His goodness and holiness. Instead, He must judge us.

Whoever believes in Him is not condemned; but whoever does not believe stands condemned already, because he has not believed in the name of God's one and only Son.
John 3:18

We realize we can never reach God through our own efforts. They do not solve the problem of our sin.

For all have sinned and come short of the glory of God.
Romans 3:23

But your iniquities have separated you from your God; your sins have hidden His face from you, so that He will not hear.
Isaiah 59:2

For the wages of sin is death, but the gift of God is eternal life in Christ Jesus our Lord.
Romans 6:23

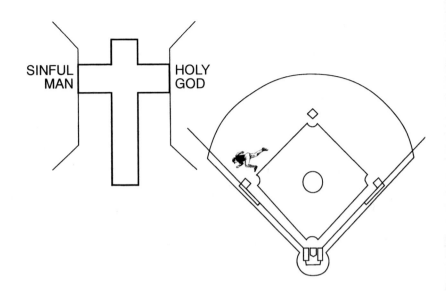

THIRD BASE is so close to scoring. Here (step 3) we under-stand that God has sent His Son, Jesus Christ, to die on the cross in payment for our sins. By His sacrifice, we may advance Home.

But God demonstrates His own love for us in this: While we were still sinners, Christ died for us.

Romans 5:8

For Christ died for sins once for all, the righteous for the unrighteous, to bring you to God.

I Peter 3:18

Jesus answered, "I am the way and the truth and the life. No one comes to the Father except through Me."

John 14:6

However, being CLOSE to Home does NOT count!

149

The Winning Run!

To score (step 4), we must personally receive Jesus Christ as Savior and Lord of our lives. We must not only realize that He died to rescue people from their sin but we must also trust Him to rescue us from our own sin. We cannot "squeeze" ourselves home any other way, and He will not force Himself upon us.

Yet to all who received Him, to those who believed in His name, He gave the right to become children of God.

John 1:12

*For it is by grace you have been saved, through faith —
and this is not from yourselves, it is the gift of God — not by works, so that no one can boast.*

Ephesians 2:8-9

Why not receive Jesus Christ as your Savior and Lord right now? Simply say: "Yes, Lord," to His offer to forgive you for your sins and to change you.

_____
(signed)

_____
(date)

Tell someone of your decision and keep studying God's Word. These things greatly strengthen you (Romans 10:9-10). You may write CROSS TRAINING PUBLISHING for fur-ther encouragement. We would be thrilled to hear of your commitment! Welcome to eternal life!

CROSS TRAINING PUBLISHING
P.O. Box 1541
Grand Island, NE 68802